Classic
SPANISH
COOKING

Classic
SPANISH
COOKING

Recipes for mastering the Spanish kitchen

ELISABETH LUARD

MQP

FOR MY BELOVED FRANCESCA
WHO LOVED THE GOOD THINGS OF LIFE
1965–1994

Published by **MQ Publications Limited**
12 The Ivories, 6–8 Northampton Street
London N1 2HY
Tel: 44 (0)20 7359 2244
Fax: 44 (0)20 7359 1616
email: mail@mqpublications.com

North American office
49 West 24th Street
New York, NY 10010
Email: information@mqpublicationsus.com

Website: www.mqpublications.com

ISBN: 1-84072-999-6

1 3 5 7 9 0 8 6 4 2

Printed and bound in China

This book contains the opinions and ideas of the author. It is intended to provide
helpful and informative material on the subjects addressed in this book and is sold
with the understanding that the author and publisher are not engaged in rendering
any kind of personal professional services in this book. The author and publisher
disclaim all responsibility for any liability, loss or risk, personal or otherwise, which is
incurred as a consequence, directly or indirectly, of the use and application of any of
the contents of this book.

contents

introduction

Behind the Spain of the costas – the tourist resorts, the sea and sand of the Mediterranean beaches, the four-lane highways and ranks of high-rise hotels – the observant visitor will be aware of an older Spain, of roads that follow the curve of valleys and lead to mountain villages shaded by Roman-planted olive trees, of a sea-horizon sparkling with the lights of wooden fishing boats night-trawling out of ancient ports whose jetties might have been cobbled together by Phoenician sailors. On the terraced hillsides can be read centuries of careful husbandry, and it's this, as well as the good earth itself, which dictates the diverse culinary traditions of a land and people already blessed by nature.

The Spaniard likes his food to look and taste of itself: meats are preferred sauced with their own juices, fish and shellfish are expected to taste of the sea, vegetables and salads are eaten as dishes in their own right. The preferred cooking oil is the fresh, untreated juice of the olive; the cooking liquid is water or wine; garlic is the pot-herb of choice. The basic cooking implements are the boiling pot, the frying pan and the *cazuela*, a shallow earthenware cooking dish tempered to withstand direct heat. High heat

is used for everything except bread-baking. The *plancha*, a heavy sheet of iron heated from beneath – the standard fitting for every modern cooker sold in Spain – is used in much the same way as the barbecue: to open shellfish, sear seafood, cook steaks, fry eggs, toast bread.

The Spanish menu begins in the marketplace, as my neighbours made clear to me in the 1970s, when I settled with my family in a remote valley in Andalusia and I took myself, my four young children and a shopping basket to market in Tarifa. Spaniards love to discuss what's for dinner – and, given half a chance and some certainty that they'll be understood, they are generous with their advice. Particularly so since, as a young mother who – although it was appreciated I could speak Spanish like a native – was handicapped by ignorance of all the things that mattered in daily life, such as how to make sure the vegetable seller was giving good weight, the fishwife wasn't selling me yesterday's sardines and the gypsy selling wild asparagus wasn't including a few stalks of the bitter stuff along with the sweet.

By ten o'clock in the morning, Tarifa, the southernmost port of the peninsula, knew what to expect of the day's rations. If the butcher had taken delivery of young beef from the Cadiz bull-ranchers that evening the town's cooking pots would fill the air with the fragrance of tripe and innards cooking with Moorish spices – the meat could safely be kept until later. When the inshore fleet came in with a particularly fine haul of silvery sardines or purple-tinged clams, or the migratory tuna – huge grey-skinned beasts – were racing though the Straits on a spring tide, the breeze carried a different flavour. Then the frying pans would breath sea scents tinged with the sharp tang of the sherry in which the shellfish are cooked, and the rich fruity olive oil which Spaniards, whenever they can afford it, use for frying and saucing their plentiful sea harvest.

Geography decides the storecupboard. The climate of the Iberian peninsula is generally benign, with sufficient rainfall in most parts and more than enough sunshine in others to produce crops throughout the year. It is almost an island, blessed with a satisfactory balance of mountain, river and plain and a long sea coast to serve as both larder and highway. A narrow neck of forbidding rock face served as a barrier against invasion from the north, whereas the heartland was protected from southern incursions by a steep line of cliff. These natural barriers allowed the natives to keep themselves to themselves, safe in their mountains and plains, until the arrival, circa AD700 across the short stretch of water which divides the western end of Europe from Africa, from the Moors, believers in the

Prophet, whose armies threatened all of Christian Europe. Once pushed back, they remained in Andalusia for seven centuries. When they left Granada, the final stronghold, the people among whom they had lived for so long had acquired a taste for sweet things, an understanding of the sophisticated art of pastrymaking and a passion for spices – most telling of all, since this was the reason Isabella of Castile sold her beautiful jewels for the price of Columbus's fragile ships.

Quality matters: the rich ate the same food as the poor, they just ate more of it. Even the poorest household will save all year for a sliver of *pata negra* ham, or the most delicate almond-and-honey *turrón*, to set on the Christmas table. While recipes are fiercely regional – no Catalan believes that any but a Catalan can cook a *fideu*, no Valencian would trust a Castilian to prepare a paella – the style remains consistent throughout the land. Tradition is respected. Even the most imaginative chef refers to what he learned as a child.

Until recent times, safe behind the barrier of the Pyrenees, isolated from the fashions and changing tastes that affected the rest of Europe, Spanish cooks preferred to concentrate on perfecting their own ingredients and culinary habits rather than take up with anything fancy or foreign. Things didn't really change after the departure of the Moors and the arrival of the New World's bounty – tomatoes, sweet peppers, marrows, maize, chocolate, potatoes, vanilla, and all the haricots – until the 1980s. The passing of the old order – Franco was as much a product of the old Spain as democracy is of the new – brought a new prosperity. Once prosperity had taken hold there came a new generation of innovative chefs, educated and literate, wielding test tubes instead of frying pans. Their ideas took hold in the restaurants of Barcelona and Madrid, spreading to those of Bilbao, Seville and all the other great cities where people enjoy the good things of life. Their effect on Spain's home cooks was, perhaps, to lighten the daily dinner, although none would attempt to copy their techniques at home. That would be foolish. As Ferran Adria, most celebrated of Spain's chemist-chefs, explained to his eager audience in London last year: 'we have to be different – no one drives a hundred kilometres to pay good money for what he can get at home'. Nevertheless, mother's home-cooking – the recipes that pop into the head of every Spaniard contemplating what to put on the table today – are also the recipes which inspired the new-wave chefs.

Spanish home cooks are a practical bunch. Market-led – call it reaction rather than recipe-cooking – the secret is that once you've made your choice, the work's half done. To know what the food you eat should look and feel and smell like in the marketplace, you need to lose your inhibitions – every Spaniard loves to prod and poke, only the foolish buy without tasting. You'll find nothing fancy in the recipes, no unobtainable ingredients – well, maybe a link of chorizo or a handful of diced serrano ham, nothing that can't be substituted if that's what's needed. And you might, if the recipe pleases you, care to acquire a few tricks: the sleight of hand required to flip a tortilla or form a neat *croqueta* – nothing a little practice can't perfect.

So here they are, the classic dishes of Spain's traditional kitchen. Good things to enjoy, a few to surprise – it all adds up to happiness – *algería* – that happy blend of sunshine, bread and wine which, together with good company, is the essence of Spain.

tapas

almendras tostadas

TOASTED ALMONDS

Although these are available commercially, almonds warm from the oven are irresistible. Prepare them fresh. The Moors planted almonds from the Jordan valley in the shady gardens of Granada's Alhambra, and Christian Spain had the good sense to appreciate the gift.

Serves 8–10

500g unskinned almonds
1 tablespoon olive oil
1 teaspoon salt
1 egg white, beaten with its own volume of water
1 tablespoon pimentón (Spanish paprika)
1 teaspoon ground coriander
1 teaspoon ground cumin

1 Preheat the oven to 180°C/350°F/Gas 4. Scald the almonds with boiling water and pop them out of their skins as soon as the water is cool enough for your fingers – my children loved the task as much as they appreciated the result.

2 Spread the skinned almonds in an oiled baking tray, shake to coat the nuts with a little oil, sprinkle with salt and roast gently for 15–20 minutes, or until just golden – shake regularly to avoid sticking, and don't let them brown. A perfectly toasted almond squeaks when you bite it. Or halve the heat and double the time – temperature is not as important as a watchful eye.

3 Allow to cool to finger-hot, toss with the egg white – a precaution which allows the salt to stick to the almond. Sprinkle with the spices, shake to coat and return to the oven for a moment to set the flavours. Leave to cool before storing in an airtight tin.

aceitunas aromatisadas

GREEN OLIVES WITH HERBS AND SPICES

This is an easy method of giving commercially prepared green olives a home-pickled flavour, particularly if made with the big green olives of Seville.

Serves 8–10

500g plain-brined green olives
3–4 garlic cloves (don't peel, chop roughly)
1 teaspoon crumbled thyme
1 teaspoon aniseed or fennel seeds
1 bitter Seville orange or 1 lemon
3–4 tablespoons sherry or white wine vinegar

1 Boil about 1 litre of water and leave it to cool. Drain the olives and mix them with the garlic, thyme and seeds.

2 Cut a thick slice from the middle of the orange or lemon and set it aside, then chop the rest of the fruit, skin and all.

3 Add the chopped fruit to the olives and pack everything in a well-scrubbed and scalded jar.

4 Add the sherry or white wine vinegar and enough water to cover, and top with the reserved slice of fruit, pushing it down to keep the olives submerged.

5 Lid tightly and leave in the fridge for at least a week to take the flavours. Keeps well in the fridge for 3–4 weeks.

NOTE: choose Spanish olives for this dish such as manzanillas, gordal or reina, if you can.

setas a la parilla

MUSHROOMS GRILLED WITH GARLIC AND PARSLEY

T*he Basques and Catalans are the mushroom fanciers of Spain. An astonishing variety of wild fungi – including boletus, chanterelles, oyster mushrooms and several members of the amanita family – are gathered in the woods and fields of the northern uplands, arriving in the market in late summer and continuing until the beginning of winter. The most popular variety is the orange-tear or saffron milk cap, a meaty mushroom gathered in pine woods, which produces a milky juice and has an alarming habit of bruising blue. All the larger specimens are suitable candidates for the grill pan. Failing a wild crop, use large open-capped cultivated mushrooms; you'll find them billed in Spanish markets as* champignons de Paris, *named for the place where they were first cultivated.*

500g large, open-capped wild or cultivated mushrooms
1 tablespoon olive oil
2 garlic cloves, finely chopped
1 tablespoon dried oregano
2 tablespoons finely chopped fresh parsley
Salt and freshly milled black pepper

1 Shake the mushrooms to evacuate any unwelcome residents, and wipe the caps – don't rinse or peel. Trim off the stalks close to the base.

2 Heat the griddle or barbecue, or if using a grill, which depends on top heat, you will have to grill the underside first.

3 Trickle the mushrooms with a little olive oil and salt lightly. Place them on the griddle or barbecue, cap-side to the heat. Grill fiercely until the juices pool in the gills.

4 Sprinkle the gills with the garlic, oregano and parsley, and plenty of freshly milled black pepper, and cook for another couple of minutes. Serve on thick slabs of toasted sourdough bread to catch the juices.

garbanzos tostados picantes

CHILLI-ROASTED CHICKPEAS

My children loved these crisp, nutty little nibbles, although I had to go easy on the chilli. Sold hot from the roasting pan at féria time in the villages of Andalusia, they are the poor man's salted almond.

Serves 8

500g dried chickpeas, soaked in cold water overnight
Olive oil for oiling
1 teaspoon chilli flakes
Sea salt

1 Preheat the oven to 150°C/300°F/Gas 2. Drain the chickpeas thoroughly and dry them in a cloth.

2 Spread them in a single layer on a lightly oiled baking sheet. Transfer to the oven and roast until dry, crisp and golden – about an hour. Shake regularly to avoid sticking. Alternatively, dry-fry the drained chickpeas over the lowest possible heat – be careful, they jump like popcorn.

3 Toss with chilli flakes and a little salt. To store, cool (don't salt or add chilli) and pack in a jar with a well-fitting lid.

patatas bravas

CHILLI POTATOES

The fiery chilli-infused oil gives the potatoes the bravery of a fighting bull. There are many versions of this recipe – tomato sauce spiked with chilli powder is one way, a sprinkle of chilli flakes is another. Here's how they make them at the Bar Tomás in Barcelona, where everyone who's anyone goes for their midday treat. You need to start at least a week ahead – the chilli needs time to impart its fire and colour to the oil.

Serves 4

Small bottle olive oil (about 200ml)
12 dried chillies
Salt
1kg floury potatoes, peeled and cut into fat fingers
Oil, for frying

1 Pour most of the olive oil into a jug. Pack the chillies into the olive-oil bottle and top up with as much oil as will fit. Seal tightly and leave for a week before using.

2 Salt the potatoes and leave them to drain in a sieve for about 10 minutes. Shake to remove excess moisture, but don't rinse.

3 Heat the oil for frying in a deep frying pan until a faint blue haze rises. Slip in the potatoes and fry gently, a batch at a time, until soft. Remove, drain, reheat the oil and fry them again, until crisp and golden. Repeat if necessary – which, depending on the choice of potato, it may well be.

4 Dress the potatoes with the chilli-infused olive oil – or hand round separately, for dipping. You can hand round a garlicky mayonnaise as well, just for good measure.

higados de pollo al vino de jerez

CHICKEN LIVERS WITH SHERRY

*S*imple, cheap and good – made with ingredients readily available in the marketplace, this is deservedly popular in the bars of Andalusia, sherry country, where the tapa tradition originated. Kidneys, sliced and given a brief soaking in a little vinegared water, take well to the same treatment.

Serves 4

350g chicken livers
2 tablespoons olive oil
1 garlic clove, finely sliced
Salt and freshly milled black pepper
1 wine glass dry sherry – fino or manzanilla (about 150ml)
1 heaped tablespoon chopped fresh parsley

1 Trim and roughly chop the chicken livers, discarding any veins and little green streaks which would make the dish taste bitter.

2 Heat the oil gently in a roomy pan – don't let it come to smoke point.

3 Add the sliced garlic and let it soften for a moment, then stir in the livers.

4 Season with a little salt and plenty of freshly milled pepper, increase the heat and toss everything over a high heat for 3–4 minutes, or until the livers are firm on the outside but still pink and soft in the middle, and the juice has evaporated to just a little oily sauce.

5 Add the dry sherry, stir in the parsley and bubble up until the steam no longer smells of alcohol – a minute or two, no more. Serve with bread for mopping.

NOTE: be careful not to overcook the chicken livers or they will become leathery and you will lose their delicate flavour.

albondigas en salsa

MEATBALLS IN TOMATO SAUCE

Tasty meatballs are the frugal housewife's stand-by. Cheap, easy to divide into small portions, they're the perfect tapa. The proportion of breadcrumbs to meat can be varied to suit your purse. Spanish housewives can buy ready-prepared meatball mince, but most prefer to pick their own combination of meat and get the butcher to put it through the mincer twice.

Serves 4

THE SAUCE

500g ripe tomatoes (canned is fine)
2 tablespoons olive oil
1 medium onion, finely chopped
1 garlic clove, finely chopped
1 red pepper, deseeded and finely chopped
1 small glass dry sherry or red wine
1 small cinnamon stick
1 bay leaf
Salt

THE MEATBALLS

350g minced meat (pork and beef is the classic combination)
1 egg, beaten
100g fresh breadcrumbs
1 garlic clove, very finely chopped
1 medium onion, very finely chopped
1 tablespoon chopped fresh parsley
1 teaspoon ground cumin
1 teaspoon ground coriander
Salt and freshly milled black pepper

TO FINISH

Flour, for dusting
2–3 tablespoons olive oil, for frying

1 Attend to the sauce first. If using fresh tomatoes, scald, skin and chop. In a small saucepan, heat the oil and fry the onion and garlic until they soften and take a little colour. Add the tomatoes, red pepper, the sherry or red wine and the cinnamon stick. Add the bay leaf and season with salt. Bubble up for a moment, then turn down the heat, and leave the sauce to simmer and reduce while you make the meatballs.

2 Work all the meatball ingredients together thoroughly – the more you work it, the better. With wet hands (keep a bowl of warm water handy for rinsing your fingers), form the mixture into little bite-sized balls. Dust them through a plateful of seasoned flour.

3 Heat the oil for frying in a roomy frying pan, slip in the meatballs and fry, turning carefully until firm and lightly browned on all sides. Add the tomato sauce, bubble up and simmer gently until the meatballs are tender, about 20 minutes. Serve with crisp lettuce leaves for scooping.

NOTE: for a more substantial meal, serve the meatballs with chunks of good country crusty bread or boiled rice.

croquetas de pollo

CHICKEN CROQUETTES

Undeniably, croquetas *are a bit more trouble than most things, but worth the effort for the pleasure of the crisp coating and the melting, creamy interior. Dexterity is required, as is patience. The basis is a thick* panada *made with a well-flavoured broth which may or may not be combined with any additional flavourings you may care to include: possibilities are diced serrano ham, crabmeat, chopped prawns or grated cheese.*

Serves 6

4 tablespoons olive oil
125g plain flour
600ml hot chicken stock
(from the *puchero* pot, or freshly made)
Salt and freshly milled black pepper
1 teaspoon ground allspice
½ teaspoon freshly grated nutmeg

TO FINISH
A plateful of seasoned flour
1–2 eggs, lightly beaten with a little water
A plateful of fresh breadcrumbs
Oil, for frying

1 Heat the oil in a small pan and stir in the flour. Lower the heat and stir for a moment or two until it looks sandy (don't let it brown). Whisk in the hot stock in a steady stream, until you have a smooth, thick sauce. Season with salt and pepper, the allspice and nutmeg. Beat the sauce over a gentle heat for 10 minutes to cook the flour. Spread in a dish, leave to cool, cover with clingfilm and set in the fridge to firm – overnight is best.

2 Form the mixture into neat little bite-sized bolsters – have a bowl of warm water beside you for dipping your hands. Dust the bolsters through the flour, coat with the egg and water mixture, and then press into the breadcrumbs to make a perfect jacket. Refrigerate for at least another hour – overnight, if possible – to set the coating. You can, if you wish, freeze a batch ready for later.

3 When you're ready to serve, heat enough oil to submerge the *croquetas* completely.

4 When the oil is faintly hazed with blue and ready to fry, slip in the *croquetas* straight from the fridge, a few at a time to avoid lowering the temperature of the oil. If the coating splits open, the oil is too hot, if it doesn't crisp and seal within a minute, it's too cool. Remove the *croquetas* with a draining spoon as soon as they're crisp and brown, and transfer to kitchen paper. Serve without delay, while they're still piping hot.

pinchitos moruños

MOORISH KEBABS

Long skewers threaded with small scraps of spiced meat – never anything but meat – rarely appear on restaurant menus unless they are aimed at tourists, but are a speciality of féria *time (the annual summer fiesta), cooked to order on a little charcoal brazier by an itinerant pedlar resplendent in a scarlet fez, a badge of office dating from the days of the Moors. In my home town of Algericas, by the Pillars of Hercules on the southern tip of Andalusia, the* pinchito *man took up position by the beer cellar – beer was the* féria-*refreshment of choice – and his* pinchitos, *the best in town, came on long, steel knitting needles which his customers were honour bound to return.*

Serves 6–8

500g lamb or pork, trimmed and diced small
2 tablespoons olive oil
1 teaspoon ground cumin
1 teaspoon ground coriander
1 teaspoon pimentón (Spanish paprika)
1 teaspoon turmeric
¹/₂ teaspoon salt
¹/₂ teaspoon freshly milled black pepper

TO SERVE
A baguette or ciabatta bread, cubed

1 Check over the meat – all the pieces should be neatly trimmed and no bigger than a baby's mouthful.

2 Combine the oil with the flavourings, and turn the mixture thoroughly with the meat. Leave in a cool place overnight to take the flavours.

3 Thread the meat onto 8 bamboo or fine metal skewers – six to seven little pieces each. If using bamboo skewers, soak them for 30 minutes first.

4 Preheat the grill or barbecue.

5 Grill the meat over a high heat, turning the skewers frequently, until well browned but still juicy. Serve on the skewers, with a cube of bread speared on the end of each so that people can pull the meat off without burning their fingers.

∽

> *" Genuine and legitimate Spanish dishes are excellent in their way, for no man nor man-cook is ever ridiculous when he does not attempt to be what he is not.... The ruin of Spanish cooks is futile attempts to imitate foreign ones. "*
>
> **Richard Ford, *Gatherings from Spain***

sardinas a la parilla

GRILLED SARDINES

This is the most popular way of preparing the fine fat sardines trawled by the inshore fleets. Fresh-caught sardines flash a brilliant rainbow of colour – green and tourquise and scarlet on silver flanks – and their eyes are bright and shiny. Don't descale the fish for grilling – the scales and the natural oil in the skin stop them sticking to the grate.

Serves 4–6

1kg whole fresh sardines
Sea salt

TO SERVE
Quartered lemons

1 Preheat the grill or a griddle – Spanish cooks use a steel plate heated from beneath.

2 Gut the sardines, leaving their heads and tails in place – easily done with your forefinger through the soft bellies – and rinse to remove the loose scales. Salt generously.

3 Lay the fish on the heat and grill fiercely, turning once, until the skin blisters black and bubbly. The thicker the fish the longer they will need, although 3–4 minutes on each side should be ample.

4 Serve one fish per tapa, with a lemon quarter. To eat, pick up the fish by the tail, holding the head with the fingers and thumb of the other hand, and eat straight down the bone, removing the fillets with your teeth. No one with any sense eats a grilled sardine with a knife and fork. You'll need chunks of bread for wiping fishy fingers.

NOTE: when buying fresh sardines look for bright eyes and a brilliant, silvery skin from which the scales have not yet become detached. Test with your fingers: the flesh should be firm and springy.

boquerones en vinagre

VINEGAR-PICKLED FRESH ANCHOVIES

Straight from the net, the anchovy looks like a small, slender sardine. Look closer and you will notice a dark stripe down the sides, a viridian sheen on the back and an apparent absence of scales: conveniently, unlike the sardine, the anchovy's scales are tiny. Both fish are plentiful throughout the region, providing the bread and butter for the inshore fishing fleets who sell them fast and cheap in the morning market. A short shelf life – the result of natural oiliness and relatively small size – means that the catch, unless salted or preserved in some other way, stays close to home. Methods of preservation – adding a few extra days rather than anything long term – involve salt or vinegar or, as here, both. Start 48 hours ahead.

Serves 4–6

500g fresh anchovies
150ml sherry or white wine vinegar
1 tablespoon sea salt
2–3 garlic cloves, finely slivered

TO FINISH
1 tablespoon olive oil
Chopped fresh flat-leaf parsley

1 Rinse the anchovies and drain thoroughly. Press your finger down the body of the fish to loosen the flesh from the bones. Holding the head firmly between finger and thumb, pull down through the belly towards the tail. The spine and ribs should slip easily through the soft flesh, gutting and splitting all in one movement. Nick the spine at the base of the tail, leaving the tail attached. Continue until all the fish are gutted and butterflied.

2 Open the fish flat and lay them flesh upwards in a single layer in a shallow dish. Mix the vinegar with 2 tablespoons of water and the salt and pour over the fish – they should be well soaked. Sprinkle with garlic, cover with foil and leave in the fridge to marinate for 48 hours. The anchovies will keep for a week in the fridge. To serve, drain and finish with a trickle of oil and a sprinkle of parsley.

boquerones fritos

FRITTERED ANCHOVIES

The freshness of the fish, the quality of the flour, the purity of the salt, and the clarity and sweetness of the oil, all contribute to the excellence of this simple dish. But the real secret lies in the ability to judge the exact moment when the oil is right for frying and the perfect moment to remove the little fish, when they are perfectly crisp but still juicy. Any small fresh fish, including cuttlefish, squid and sea anemones, can be given the same treatment.

Serves 4

500g fresh anchovies (or small sardines)
4 tablespoons strong bread flour
1 tablespoon fine-ground semolina
1 teaspoon sea salt, crushed
Oil, for frying (a mixture of olive and sunflower is perfect)

TO SERVE
Quartered lemons

1 Rinse and gut the little fish – just run your finger down the soft belly and remove the innards. Behead them or not, as you please. Very small fish don't need gutting or beheading. Anchovies don't need scaling, although sardines, even very small ones, always do. Rinse under running water in a colander, but don't dry.

2 Mix the flour with the semolina and salt, and spread on a plate. Pick up the fish by their tails in groups of three or four, depending on size, holding them between your forefinger and thumb in a fan shape. Flip the fans through the flour, first one side, then the other, making sure the tails are firmly stuck together with flour.

3 Meanwhile, heat the oil for frying in a frying pan – you need just enough oil to submerge the fish (fish-frying oil cannot be re-used). When the oil is lightly hazed with blue, lay in the fish-fans head first, releasing the pinched-together tails just before you burn your fingers. Fry only two to three fans at a time so that the temperature remains high. Fry quickly, turning once, until the coating is crisp and pale golden. The little bunch of tails will be exquisitely crunchy. Transfer to kitchen paper to drain. Serve with quartered lemons.

pimientos asados con anchoas

ROAST RED PEPPERS WITH ANCHOVIES

The sweet, soft flesh of the peppers perfectly complements the salty fillets of anchovy – the best are the chewy little morsels packed straight from the cold waters of the Bay of Biscay in the canneries of Asturias and Galicia. Choose plump, ripe, red bell peppers or the scarlet triangular peppers they grow in the sunny fields of Rioja in among the vineyards. You can also buy specially prepared red peppers in cans – look for pimientos del piquillo, *a bargain, as it happens.*

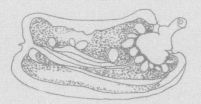

Serves 4

4 red peppers
2 tablespoons extra virgin olive oil
1 can salt-pickled anchovies in oil, drained

1 Turn the whole peppers on the end of a knife in a flame until the skin blisters and blackens. Or roast them in an oven preheated to 240°C/475°F/Gas 9 for 15–20 minutes, turning them halfway through.

2 Pop the peppers in a plastic bag to sweat and cool. Scrape off the skin gently with a sharp knife. Remove the seeds and cut the flesh into triangles or ribbons, depending on the original shape of the pepper. Arrange the peppers in a single layer on a plate and trickle with a little olive oil. Arrange the anchovies decoratively over the top.

SERVING SUGGESTION: accompany with plenty of crusty bread to mop up all the delicious juices.

calamares a la romana

FRITTERED SQUID

Squid (calamares) *and cuttlefish* (chocos) *are both suitable for the treatment – a simple matter of flipping the prepared fish through flour to give it a light coating that crisps in the fryer. To prepare* calamar *or squid, separate the body from the cap and discard the supporting 'bone' which, in the squid, looks like a long sheet of clear plastic, and in the cuttlefish is a chalky oval disc, a treat much appreciated by captive canaries. The caps of larger specimens should be sliced into rings, and the bodies, once you have discarded the soft innards and the eye section, similarly sliced. The tentacles can be left as little bunches, although those from larger specimens should be scraped to remove the spiky little 'toenails' which support the suckers. Small specimens (no bigger than will fit into a teaspoon) can be fried whole, just as they come from the sea.*

Serves 4–6

**500g prepared squid or cuttlefish, sliced into rings, tentacles
left whole
About 4 tablespoons strong bread flour
1 tablespoon semolina
Oil, for frying (a mixture of olive and sunflower is good)**

TO SERVE
**Sea salt
Quartered lemons**

1 Rinse, drain and shake the fish to remove excess moisture
(don't dry it completely).

2 Spread the flour mixed with the semolina on a plate (no salt).
Working quickly, dust the fish through the flour a few pieces at
a time – the surface should be damp enough for the flour to form
a coating – drop into a sieve and shake to remove excess flour.

3 Meanwhile, heat the oil in a deep-fryer or heavy frying pan.
Test the temperature of the oil with a bread cube: it's ready
for frying when bubbles form around the edge immediately and
the crumb turns golden within a few seconds. Drop the coated
fish into the hot oil quickly in batches and fry until golden and
crisp, turning once. Transfer to kitchen paper to drain.

4 Serve piping hot and without reheating (reheating makes
cephalopods rubbery), lightly salted and accompanied by
lemon quarters.

gambas a la parilla

SALT-GRILLED PRAWNS

Choose large, raw prawns, preferably ones with the heads left on, a guarantee of freshness since nothing goes off more quickly than a prawn head. Your nose will tell you if they're as they should be – housewives in Algeciras, my market town when I lived in Andalusia, simply shoved a finger in the juices in the prawn box and tasted the brine. If the flavour was noticeably salty, the boats had been too long at sea and the fishermen had been obliged to use salt as well as ice to preserve the catch.

Serves 4–6

500g large raw prawns, unpeeled, with heads on
Olive oil
Coarse salt

TO SERVE
Quartered lemons

⚮

1 Rub the prawns lightly with oil and dredge generously with
coarse salt – salt on the shell enhances the natural sweetness of
the flesh inside.

2 Preheat the grill or cook on a griddle – the heat should be
fierce enough to blacken the shells a little. Turn once, allowing
2–3 minutes each side. Lemon quarters should accompany. The
juices from the head are exquisite – don't be shy, crush the heads
between your teeth and suck.

NOTE: this is quite messy, so provide finger bowls and napkins
for guests to wipe their fingers and mouths clean afterwards.

tortillitas de camarónes

SHRIMP FRITTERS

These crisp little fritters are sold hot from the frying vat on every street corner of the windswept port of Cadiz, where they're made with tiny jumping shrimps, camarones, *netted in the long sandy shallows on the edge of the salt flats beyond the town. You can replace the chickpea flour with bread flour plus a tablespoon of semolina.*

Serves 4–6

4 tablespoons chickpea flour
½ teaspoon bicarbonate of soda
½ teaspoon salt
2 tablespoons olive oil
¼ teaspoon pimentón (Spanish paprika)
1 tablespoon chopped fresh parsley
1 tablespoon very finely chopped onion
125g whole tiny shrimps, or peeled shrimps, finely chopped
Oil, for frying

1 Sieve the chickpea flour, bicarbonate of soda and salt into a bowl, and gradually blend in 6 tablespoons water and the oil until you have a thin batter. Stir in the pimentón or paprika, parsley and onion. Fold in the chopped shrimps.

2 Heat two fingers' depth of oil in a frying pan. When it is lightly smoking, drop in the shrimp batter by the tablespoonful – not too many at time or the oil temperature will drop. Fry until golden and crisp, turning once. Flatten the fritters with a draining spoon as they cook – the batter must be well-spread out so that the fritters crisp right through. Transfer to kitchen paper to drain and serve.

gambas pilpil

PRAWNS WITH GARLIC AND CHILLI

Tapa bars which specialize in these mouth-scalding preparations provide customers with little wooden forks so they don't burn their lips. Angulas, *baby eels, are prepared in the same way, as are hake throats,* kokochas, *the fatty little piece under the chin, a speciality of the Basque country, where hake,* merluza, *is the national dish.*

Serves 4

350g peeled raw prawns
4 tablespoons olive oil
1 garlic clove, sliced
1 teaspoon small dried chillies, deseeded
Sea salt

1 Pick over the prawns and remove any stray whiskers.

2 The important thing about this simple dish is that the prawns must be sizzling hot when they are served, ideally in the dish in which they are cooked. With this in mind, choose small individual casseroles capable of resisting a flame. Alternatively, use a frying pan to cook the prawns, and heat individual ramekin dishes in the oven for serving.

3 Heat the oil. When lightly hazed with blue, add the garlic and chillies. Reheat until it sizzles, then add the prawns and let them cook. They'll turn opaque almost immediately. Serve as soon as the oil spits and bubbles, in the heated ramekins or their individual casseroles, with bread for mopping up the fiery oil. Hand the sea salt round separately.

NOTE: you will need raw prawns or shrimps, fresh or frozen, for this dish – precooked won't do.

almejas en vino de jerez

CLAMS IN SHERRY

Bivalves have a relatively long shell life, surviving for as long as they can keep water in their shells – hence the need to reject those with cracked shells or which remain closed when cooked. Spanish housewives expect to buy the shellfish live in the shell, the only guarantee of freshness.

Serves 4–6

1kg live bivalves – clams, cockles, mussels, razor shells
2 tablespoons olive oil
2 garlic cloves, finely chopped
1 large glass dry sherry or white wine
2 tablespoons chopped fresh parsley
Salt and freshly milled black pepper
A little sugar

1 Wash the shellfish in plenty of cold water, checking over and discarding any which are broken or weigh unusually heavy – they're probably dead and filled with sand. Also discard any that do not close when sharply tapped.

2 Heat the oil in a saucepan, add the garlic and let it soften for a moment. Tip in the shellfish, add the sherry or wine and the parsley. Season with salt, pepper and a little sugar, and turn up the heat. As soon as steam rises, cover with a lid and leave to cook, shaking the pan to redistribute the shells. Allow 3–4 minutes for all the shells to open – check and turn them over if necessary. Discard any shells that remain closed.

3 Remove the pan from the heat as soon as the shells are open and serve straight from the pot – never mind if they cool down to room temperature, which happens very swiftly. Don't reheat or they'll be rubbery. Leftovers can be served with a little dressing of chopped tomato, parsley and onion.

SERVING SUGGESTION: serve in deep plates and eat with your fingers. Provide plenty of bread for mopping up the juices.

atún en adobo

VINEGAR-PICKLED TUNA

This is one of the economical little preparations originally devised in the days before refrigeration (a comparatively recently development – no more than a century old) that was intended to preserve the fisherman's catch for a little longer, particularly in summer. So good, it remains on the menu. The same treatment can be applied to any firm-fleshed fish which is suitable for cutting into chunks: swordfish steaks or mackerel chopped across the bone work well.

Serves 4

500g tuna steaks
Salt
1 heaped tablespoon strong bread flour
2–3 tablespoons olive oil

THE MARINADE
1 medium onion, finely sliced
1 garlic clove, crushed
1 small carrot, sliced
1 tablespoon chopped fresh parsley
1 bay leaf, torn
1 teaspoon dried oregano or marjoram
6 peppercorns, roughly crushed
4 tablespoons sherry vinegar (or any wine vinegar)

1 Cut the tuna into bite-sized chunks. Sprinkle with salt and dust with the flour. Fry gently in the oil until golden and firm (use your thumb to test that the flesh is firm). Transfer to a serving dish, arranging the chunks in a single layer.

2 Reheat the oil remaining in the pan – you may need a little more – and add the onion, garlic and carrot. Fry gently for a few moments so that the flavours blend. Add the herbs, peppercorns, vinegar and a splash of water. Bubble fiercely for a few minutes, then pour the marinade over the fish. Turn the pieces gently, cover loosely with a clean cloth, and leave overnight in a cool place. Ready to eat in a day, better in two.

ensalada de mariscos

SEAFOOD SALAD

A versatile composition which makes use of whatever the fishing fleet has landed and is going cheap in the market. Shellfish – mussels, cockles and other bivalves – should be steamed open in their shells and shucked. Crustaceans – prawns, langoustines and shrimp – should be cooked and peeled. Cephalopods – cuttlefish, octopus and squid – should be sliced, cooked and drained. Possible additions include cubes of firm-fleshed fish – tuna, swordfish and monkfish – briefly steamed in very little salted water. A combination of at least three different varieties is good. If there's a shortage of fish, include little cubes of cooked potato.

Serves 4–6

500g mixed cooked seafood (shelled if appropriate)
3 spring onions or fresh green garlics, thickly sliced
1 red or green pepper, deseeded and diced
1 garlic clove, chopped
1 tablespoon chopped fresh flat-leaf parsley
4 tablespoons olive oil
1 tablespoon sherry or white wine vinegar
Salt and freshly milled black pepper

1 Pick over the seafood and make sure all the pieces are more or less the same size. Toss with the rest of the ingredients.

2 Leave the seafood salad in a cool place to marinate for a few hours or overnight.

3 Serve with cos lettuce leaves for scooping and plenty of bread for mopping.

NOTE: green garlic (or as it is sometimes called, new season garlic) are freshly harvested garlic bulbs in which the cloves have not yet been allowed to develop – a process which happens when the garlics are allowed to dry. It can be roasted or sliced and used in salads.

The tapa – directly translated the word means lid – is generally presented as something to pop on a glass to keep the flies out of the wine, although there seems no particular reason why flies on the food should be considered preferable. Although tapas only officially appeared about a century ago – they were first recorded in Seville – the tradition is linked to a far older one: that of hospitality and the desire to honour a guest. '*Algo para picar?*' – something to nibble? – is the question that always accompanies the offer of a glass of wine in Andalusia. The habit has spread with varying degrees of generosity to other parts of Spain. In Madrid, where evening tapas are an institution, people order plates of suitable foods for sharing, and each tapa is known for a particular speciality. The same rule applies in Seville and the other major cities of the south, with fresh fish the favourite. Sardines and anchovies – cheap, delicious and landed daily – are the most likely to be offered free. Olives and bread always come free, unless you're on one of the costas in a clip-joint aimed solely at tourists. The further you are from the tourist centres, the more likely it is that the tapa will be included in the price of a glass of wine.In the university cities of the north – Bilbao in particular – students generally pool their resources and make the rounds of the tapa bars until they run out of money.

Tapas are defined by quantity: a single portion of a luxury such as *jamón serrano* provides a tapa to share between four; a single tapa is as much as will fit on a saucer or one of the specially made little boat-shaped dishes: a single meatball with its sauce, three little anchovies fried crisp in a fan, a spoonful of whatever's on the menu in the restaurant at the back. The composition of a free tapa is dependent on what's readily available and cheap – preferably free. If there are snails at the bottom of your garden, snails is the tapa you will offer your guests. If the fishermen have returned with more sardines than they can sell, the local bar will serve grilled sardines with the traveller's glass of wine. In ham-curing areas, the tapa is likely to involve tripe and innards, or maybe tails and ears, or crisp curls of pork crackling, puffed and brown and sizzling hot from the pan. It's not all meat: there might be a little taste of broad beans cooked in oil with sherry, a plate of crisp chips doused with chilli oil, a cube of juicy tortilla.

In addition to these good things, there's a variable galaxy of larder treats that can be produced in an emergency: salted anchovies, wind-dried tuna, ready-roasted red peppers from Rioja, slices of chorizo or *morcilla*, toasted almonds, chilli-roasted chickpeas, a square of good fresh country bread spread with *manteca colorado* – pork dripping coloured with pimentón. It's a matter of honour not to serve the same tapa twice to the same person. When all else fails, however, there's always a spoonful of Russian salad, a dab of chickpeas from the *puchero* saved from the day before. Tapas, it must be said, offer the cheapest and most convenient way to sample what any region has to offer – although these days for the best, you have to be prepared to part with your money.

light
soups

gazpacho

CHILLED TOMATO AND GARLIC SOUP

In its modern form, this is a refreshing chilled tomato soup. In its land of origin, it's simply a way of making last week's bread palatable by soaking it with fresh water and flavouring it with a sprinkle of vinegar, garlic and a thread of oil. The texture – depending on the degree of dilution – changes with the season. In summer, heavily diluted, it's treated as a refreshment – Andalusians keep a jug of it in the fridge – whereas in winter, it's made with boiling water and eaten with a spoon, much like a porridge. All this has changed in modern times, when it has turned into a tomato-based soup in which bread is simply used as a light thickening. Onion makes it vulnerable to fermentation, so is not usually included. In Cordoba, it's called salmorejo and takes the form of a thick, spoonable purée served with all the extras: chopped serrano ham, hard-boiled egg, chopped tomato, garlic, cucumber. Here's the modern version; embellish it as you please.

Serves 4

2 slices day-old bread (about 50g)
2 tablespoons wine vinegar
2 garlic cloves, crushed
2 tablespoons olive oil
1 small cucumber or half a large one, peeled and
roughly chopped
1kg ripe tomatoes, skinned, deseeded and chopped
1 green pepper, cored and deseeded, roughly chopped
Salt and a little sugar

❧

1 Put the bread to soak in a few tablespoons of ice-cold spring water with the vinegar and garlic. Pound the mixture in a mortar or drop everything in the liquidizer and process to a purée. Add the oil and remaining vegetables. Add ice-cold spring water until you have the consistency you like – thick or thin, depending on whether you mean to serve it as a refreshment or a soup. Adjust the seasoning with salt and a little sugar. Transfer to a jug and cover securely. Set in a cold larder or the fridge for 2–3 hours, or until well chilled. No ice – it just dilutes the flavour and replaces it with the taste of the fridge.

2 As a refreshment, serve in a chilled glass. As a first-course soup, ladle into bowls and hand round any extras separately. Choose from diced bread croutons fried in a little olive oil (only worth it if you make your own), chopped hard-boiled egg, diced *jamon serrano*, cucumber, peppers, tomato or mild Spanish onion.

ajo blanco

WHITE GAZPACHO

A sophisticated summer refresher from Granáda, where it's also known as gazpacho blanco, white gazpacho, is made with an infusion of almond milk heavily perfumed with garlic. The Moors can be held responsible for its inclusion in the repertoire. You don't need much of it: it has a kick like a mule. I like to serve it in a little tumbler with another tumbler of red gazpacho and a glass of chilled dry sherry.

Serves 6–8

1 slice yesterday's bread, crusts removed
100g blanched almonds
2 garlic cloves, peeled
1 tablespoon olive oil
1 tablespoon white wine vinegar
Salt and sugar

TO FINISH
A few small white grapes, peeled and deseeded

1 Put the bread, almonds, garlic, oil, vinegar and half a litre of cold water into the blender, and process thoroughly. Add enough water – another half litre or so – to give the consistency of thin milk. Season with salt and sugar to taste. Transfer to a jug and chill thoroughly.

2 To serve, pour into small bowls or glasses, and try to float a couple of grapes on top of each serving. Mine always drop to the bottom. No matter. It'll make a nice surprise at the end. Warn participants this is a high-garlic area.

caldo gallego

SOUP WITH BEANS AND GREENS

This robust first-course soup is usually made with turnip tops (grelos) rather than cabbage. Chard is a possible alternative, although the flavour is a little bland unless you include a handful of rocket or other mustardy leaves. Traditionally, a bowl of caldo provided Galicia's rural households with their daily intake of fresh greens. Without it, the diet would be short on vegetables – important when considering the balance of a meal. Here's how they like it in the inland city of Orense in the cold uplands close to the Portuguese border.

Serves 4–6

250g white haricot or butter beans, soaked overnight
2 tablespoons pork lard or diced fat bacon
500g tender young turnips, chunked
Salt and freshly milled black pepper
1kg potatoes, peeled and chunked
1 smallish green cabbage or 500g spring greens, finely sliced

1 Drain the beans and put them in a roomy flameproof pot with enough water to cover to a depth of two fingers' width. Bring to the boil, skim off the grey foam which rises, and add the lard or bacon. Turn down the heat, loosely cover with a lid and leave to bubble gently for about 1½ hours, or until the beans are tender, adding more boiling water as necessary – the level of water should remain roughly constant. Season with salt and pepper.

2 Ladle half the broth into another pot, bring to the boil and add the turnips. Return the broth to the boil and add the potatoes. Simmer for 15 minutes or so, until the vegetables are nearly soft. Add the cabbage or spring greens to the same pot, bring all back to the boil, cover and cook for another 6–10 minutes, until the vegetables are soft and the cabbage is tender but still green. Set the two pots on the table for people to combine their own.

sopa de mariscos con vino de jerez

SHELLFISH SOUP WITH SHERRY

You need fresh raw shellfish on the shell – ready cooked won't do. If this proves impossible, a combination of firm-fleshed white fish – monkfish, swordfish – and oysters gives good results. Shuck the oysters first, naturally, and slip them in right at the end to heat through.

Serves 4

500g soup fish (or ask your fishmonger for bones and heads)
1 glass dry sherry (about 200ml)
1 onion, quartered but unpeeled
1 carrot, roughly chopped
3–4 fresh parsley sprigs
1–2 bay leaves
½ teaspoon crushed peppercorns
1 teaspoon salt
12 saffron threads, soaked in a little water
1kg fresh shellfish, well washed to remove sand
1 tablespoon diced serrano ham
1 tablespoon pimentón (Spanish paprika)

1 teaspoon grated lemon zest
1 teaspoon finely chopped garlic
1 tablespoon chopped fresh parsley

1 Rinse the soup fish (or the bones and heads) and transfer to a roomy pan with about 1 litre of water and the sherry. Bring to the boil. Skim off the foam. Add the onion, carrot, aromatics and salt. Return everything to the boil, turn the heat down immediately, and simmer for 20 minutes – no longer or the broth will be bitter.

2 Strain the broth and return it to the pan. Stir in the saffron and its water – first crushed either with the back of the spoon or given a quick whizz in the liquidizer. Reheat to just boiling, and add the shellfish, ham and pimentón. Return everything to the boil, cover and cook until the shellfish open, about 3–4 minutes. Remove from the heat, taste and adjust the seasoning. Finish with a sprinkle of lemon zest, chopped garlic and parsley. Serve without reheating.

NOTE: if you use fish heads for the stock be careful to remove the gills or the stock will become bitter.

"Of soup and love, the first is the best."

Spanish saying

First-course soups, the second act of the traditional Spanish meal, can be distinguished from the main-course soup – substantial one-pot meals based on pulses, highly regional, of which the broth is often served before the solids – by the absence of large pieces of meat, although meat of some kind is usually the basis of the broth. These light soups act as a chaser for the salty appetizers – serrano ham, chorizo, small frittered fish – clearing the palate for the main dish. The most widely appreciated of these broths is a clear consommé with or without the addition of noodles or rice – a group which includes 15–minute soup, *sopa de cuarto de hora* – and vegetable-thickened broths such as the Basque leek soup, *purrusalda*. Also within the category are clear fish soups made with bones and heads, often coloured and flavoured with saffron and finished with shellfish. In addition, although often served as a refreshment, there are two Andalusian chilled soups from ancient recipes inherited from the days of the Moors. *Ajo blanco*, a garlicky white gazpacho made with almond milk, and the modern tomato-based gazpacho which has largely, in these days of greater prosperity, replaced the traditional bread porridge from which it acquired its name.

sopa de ajo

GARLIC SOUP

Garlic, the blessed Allium sativum *used by wise women to discourage the devil and by the church to frighten the wise women, grows wild around the shores of the Mediterranean. More than a flavouring, it's a philosophy, a declaration of otherness, a way of life. Here, in a simple soup which is given to invalids and babies as well as their elderly relatives, it's cooked to a gentle sweetness which soothes the spirit and calms the stomach.*

Serves 4

6 tablespoons olive oil
6 thick slices robust country bread, cut into cubes
12 fine fat garlic cloves, crushed
1 tablespoon pimentón (Spanish paprika)
About 1 litre chicken stock or water
Salt and freshly milled black pepper
4 eggs

1 Preheat the oven to 180°C/350°F/Gas 4. Warm the oil in a heavy pan and drop in the bread cubes and the garlic as soon as it's hot enough to fry. Fry gently and patiently until the garlic softens and the bread is golden – don't let it brown. Stir in the pimentón or paprika and add the stock or water. Season lightly, bring to the boil, cover and cook for 5 minutes, or until the bread is spongy and has soaked up most of the juice.

2 Meanwhile, heat four small one-person earthenware casseroles (*cazuelas*) either on the stove or in the oven. Ladle in the soupy bread with its broth, and crack in the eggs – one for each casserole. You can return them to the oven for the eggs to set, or serve immediately, for people to stir the egg into the boiling soup.

purrusalda

LEEK AND POTATO SOUP

This, a robust country soup thick with leeks, is, as its name suggests, a winter warmer from the Basque Country. The broth is enriched with garlic-infused olive oil. Very simple and good.

Serves 4–6

8–10 large leeks, with their green tops
100ml olive oil
4 garlic cloves, halved
4 medium potatoes, peeled and diced
Ground allspice or nutmeg (optional)
2 tablespoons chopped fresh parsley (optional)
Salt and freshly milled black pepper

1 Bring 1½ litres of water to the boil, and salt lightly. Meanwhile, trim the leeks, discarding the tough green parts, and slice lengthways into long, thin ribbons. Stir the leeks into the water as soon as it bubbles. Turn down the heat and leave to simmer for 20 minutes, until the leeks have melted into the broth.

2 Meanwhile, warm the oil in a small pan and fry the garlic until soft and golden – remove the pan from the heat as soon as they begin to brown. Reserve.

3 Add the potatoes to the leek pot, return all to the boil, turn down the heat and cook gently for another 15–20 minutes, or until the potatoes soften and collapse. Mash a little to thicken. Stir in the garlic and oil and bubble up again to amalgamate the oil and the broth. Taste and adjust the seasoning – maybe add a little ground allspice or nutmeg. Or stir in a thick shower of parsley: the Basques have a passion for parsley.

4 Serve as a starter, or as a light main course with bread and cheese – maybe a slice of smoked *Idiazabal*, a creamy, refreshingly sharp sheep's cheese, the pride of the region.

sopa de picadillo

HAM AND EGG SOUP

The usual basis for this simple soup – also known as 15-minute soup, sopa de cuarto de hora, *because it's so quickly prepared – is the broth from the* puchero, *Andalusia's version of the universal boiled dinner. The mint gives it a Moorish edge.*

Serves 4

1 litre chicken broth
2 tablespoons short-grain rice
4 tablespoons chopped serrano ham
2 hard-boiled eggs, chopped
1 tablespoon finely chopped fresh parsley
1 tablespoon finely chopped fresh mint

1 Bring the broth, rice and ham to the boil in a saucepan. Turn down the heat and simmer for 15 minutes, or until the rice is nearly tender.

2 Add the chopped egg to the saucepan and simmer for another 2–3 minutes. Remove from the heat and stir in the parsley and mint. That's all. Simple, isn't it?

NOTE: to cook hard-boiled eggs, place the unshelled eggs in a pan of boiling water. Return the water to the boil, turn down the heat and simmer for 10 minutes. Transfer the eggs to cold water and leave for another 10 minutes, until cool. The yolk and white should be completely set.

eggs

tortilla española

POTATO TORTILLA

Call it egg and chips, Spanish-style: same ingredients, different method of attack. You find this soft-centred egg-cake in pride of place, the thicker and bigger the better, in every tapa bar. It's the busy housewife's stand-by for any meal, from breakfast to dinner. Children take it to school for lunch. Toothless grannies thrive on it. Opinions vary about the inclusion of parsley and onion; I leave the first one out and put the second one in. The shape of the potatoes is also a matter for discussion: some like them cut into thin rounds, others like them chip-shaped or cubed. Feel free to suit yourself.

Serves 4

About 750g potatoes (allow 1 medium potato per egg)
Olive oil, for frying
1 tablespoon finely chopped onion
4 large free-range eggs
½ teaspoon salt

1 Peel and dice or slice the potatoes. Heat enough oil to submerge the potatoes completely – choose a frying pan in which you would usually cook a one-person omelette. Add the potatoes and fry gently until absolutely soft – don't let them colour. Add the chopped onion for the last few minutes, just long enough to soften it.

2 Transfer the potato and onion to a sieve placed over a bowl to catch the drippings. Allow to cool to finger temperature. Lightly beat the eggs with the salt. Stir in the potatoes. At this point, the volume of the cooked potato should equal the volume of egg.

3 Pour all but a tablespoon of the oil out of the pan and add the drippings from the bowl (the rest of the oil can be used again). Reheat the pan and tip in the egg and potato mixture. Prod down the potato so that they are all submerged. Use a fork to pull the egg into the middle as soon as the edges begin to set. Fry gently, loosely lidded, until the surface no longer looks absolutely runny. The heat should be low or the base will burn before the egg is cooked. Don't overcook it – the centre should remain juicy. If the heat is too high, the egg will be leathery.

4 Place a clean plate over the pan, and invert the whole thing with one quick movement so that the tortilla lands juicy side up. Be brave: it's no harder than flipping a pancake. Reheat the pan with a little more oil, and slip the tortilla, soft side downwards, back into the pan and set the other side. When the underside is done, reverse the tortilla back onto the plate and pat off the excess oil with kitchen paper. Serve at room temperature, cut into neat wedges or cubes.

tortilla valenciana

AUBERGINE TORTILLA

Aubergines, the poor man's meat, provide the bulk in this version of Spanish tortilla which predates the arrival of the New World's potatoes. The spicing is distinctly Moorish: long after the departure of the caliphs from the land they called the gateway to Paradise, the cooks of Andalusia have never lost their taste for the flavours of the East.

Serves 2–4

4 large free-range eggs
4 tablespoons olive oil
4 garlic cloves, roughly chopped
2 firm, fat aubergines, diced
1 tablespoon ground cumin
1 teaspoon ground cinnamon
1 teaspoon ground coriander
Salt and freshly milled black pepper

1 Crack the eggs into a bowl and beat lightly to blend.

2 Warm the oil in a frying pan. Add the chopped garlic and fry gently for a moment or two – just enough to soften. Add the aubergine cubes and salt lightly: they'll drink up the oil like little sponges. Fry steadily, stirring, until the oil is released back into the pan and the aubergine cubes soften and brown a little. Drain off the excess oil and reserve.

3 Add the spices and pepper; fry for a moment longer, cover and leave to cook very gently in its own juices for 15–20 minutes. Mash thoroughly and allow to cool to finger heat.

4 Stir the mashed aubergine into the eggs and blend thoroughly.

5 Heat a small frying pan – whatever you would normally use to prepare a one-person omelette – and add the reserved oil as soon as the pan is good and hot. Tip in the egg mixture and turn down the heat. Pull the sides to the middle as soon as the edges begin to set. Cover loosely and cook gently for 5–6 minutes, or until the top begins to look softly set.

6 Place a plate on top of the pan – it should completely cover the edges – and reverse the whole thing so that the tortilla ends up soft side down on the plate. Reheat the pan (you may need a little more oil), and slip in the tortilla to cook the other side. Neaten the edges as it cooks – a couple more minutes – and transfer to a warm plate. Pat with kitchen paper to absorb excess oil.

SERVING SUGGESTION: particularly good with a sharp little sauce of fresh white curd cheese whisked with a spoonful of honey.

tortilla catalana

BEAN AND CHORIZO TORTILLA

A spicy winter tortilla, a speciality of Catalonia, made with leftovers from the bean pot and a handful of diced butifarra negro, *black pudding spiced with cinnamon, cloves and nutmeg (rather than the more usual oregano and pimentón). If you can't find butifarra, use chorizo. Beans – haricot or butter beans – can replace the chickpeas. It all depends on what's available.*

Serves 4

2 tablespoons olive oil
2 tablespoons diced *butifarra* or chorizo
6 tablespoons cooked chickpeas, well-drained
4 large free-range eggs
Salt and freshly milled black pepper

1 Warm a tablespoon of olive oil in a one-person omelette pan. Fry the sausage for a few minutes until the edges brown and fat runs. Add the chickpeas and warm them through.

2 Beat the eggs lightly with salt and pepper. Mix in the contents of the frying pan. Wipe the pan and heat the rest of the oil. Tip in the egg mixture, stir to blend the ingredients as the egg sets a little, and cook gently until it takes the form of a thick pancake, loosely covered, neatening the sides as the curds firm up. Turn it by reversing the whole panful onto a plate so that the contents end up soft-side down.

3 Slip it back into the hot pan (add a little more oil if necessary), to allow the other side to set – a couple of minutes. The whole operation should be very gentle and take no more than 7–8 minutes in all.

revuelto de setas

SCRAMBLED EGGS WITH MUSHROOMS

Eggs scrambled with olive oil are the perfect way to stretch wild gatherings such as the saffron milk cap, a pine-wood fungus which, though it oozes milky juices and bruises an alarming navy blue, speaks volumes to the Catalan. A revuelto can feature any firm-fleshed wild fungi – porcini, chanterelles, hedgehog fungi (the ones which have little teeth instead of gills), oyster mushrooms. In spring, a fresh-flavoured revuelto is made with asparagus sprue – chewy little green shoots gathered from beneath the prickly bushes of the native wild asparagus, which come, somewhat disconcertingly, in two forms, bitter and mild, and I have never been able to work out how to tell the difference without tasting.

Serves 3–4

4 tablespoons olive oil
1–2 garlic cloves, finely chopped
About 350g fresh woodland mushrooms (saffron milk caps,
porcini, chanterelles), sliced
2 tablespoons diced serrano ham
6 eggs
1 tablespoon finely chopped fresh parsley
Salt and freshly milled black pepper

1 In an earthenware *cazuela* or a heavy iron pan, heat the oil and add the garlic. Allow to sizzle for a minute or two until the garlic softens, then add the mushrooms and ham. Sprinkle with a little salt, turn up the heat until the mushrooms absorb the oil, then turn down the heat and cook gently until the fungi yield up their juices and begin to fry again.

2 Meanwhile, lightly beat the eggs with the parsley, and season with a little salt and plenty of pepper. Stir the eggs into the mushrooms, and continue to stir over a gentle heat until the eggs form soft curds – no more than a minute or two. Remove the cooking implement from the heat just before the egg sets. Stir again and serve in the cooking dish, with plenty of crusty bread for mopping.

huevos al plato con pimientos

HAM AND EGGS WITH RED PEPPERS

*A*n *easy evening meal for townies who have been out on a
tapa bar round with friends after work. Spaniards prefer
to lunch prodigiously and take a relatively light supper.*

Serves 4–6

**2 red peppers
2–3 tablespoons olive oil
4 slices serrano ham
8 eggs
Freshly milled black pepper**

1 For the proper presentation of this simple recipe, you will need four one-person *cazuelas* (shallow earthenware dishes, used in Spain for frying) which have been tempered (see note below) to withstand direct heat.

2 Roast the peppers by holding them in direct heat, speared on the end of a knife, or under a hot grill, until the skin burns and blackens. Pop then in a bag (paper or plastic), wait 10 minutes for the skin to loosen, then peel with your fingers. Deseed and cut into strips.

3 Pour a tablespoon of oil into each individual *cazuela* and place them carefully on direct heat. When the oil is smoking hot, lay in the peppers and a slice of ham and crack in the eggs – 2 to each cazuela. Cook for 3–4 minutes to set the white. Give each dish a turn of the pepper mill and then serve. The eggs will continue to cook in their dish.

NOTE: to temper a cazuela, rub the surface inside and out with garlic (the inside is glazed, the outside unglazed), fill the cazuela with water and place it over direct heat – gas or electric, or any open flame. Bring to the boil and boil steadily until the water has completely evaporated. If the cazuela doesn't crack now, it never will. If it does, you'll have to get another – but they're extremely cheap and you can always drop the cracked bits in the bottom of the flower pot when you're potting up your geraniums.

piperrada

SCRAMBLED EGGS WITH ONION AND AUBERGINE

Eggs scrambled into a juicy combination of aubergine, tomato and garlic cooked in oil, a speciality of the Basque country. The vegetables can be prepared ahead and the eggs scrambled in at the last minute.

Serves 4

4 tablespoons olive oil
1 onion, finely sliced into half-moons
1 garlic clove, finely chopped
1 aubergine, diced
1 red pepper, diced
1 large tomato, skinned, deseeded and chopped
4 free-range eggs, lightly beaten to blend
Salt and chilli powder

1 Heat half the oil in an earthenware *cazuela* or heavy iron pan. Add the sliced onion and chopped garlic, salt lightly and cook gently for at least 20 minutes until they soften and brown a little – don't let them burn. Remove to a sieve placed over a bowl to catch the drippings.

2 Reheat the pan with the remaining oil and add the diced aubergine. Cook until soft and lightly caramelized at the edges (return the drippings to the pan as soon as they are available). Remove the aubergine and reserve.

3 Add the pepper and turn it in the hot oil until it has softened and taken a little colour. Add the tomato and bubble up for a minute or two, until the flesh begins to collapse. Return the reserved vegetables to the pan and reheat. Season with salt and a little chilli powder.

4 Fold the eggs into the vegetables and stir over a gentle heat while the eggs form soft curds, about 1–2 minutes, no more. Remove from the heat immediately.

SERVING SUGGESTION: provide toasted country bread and a garlic clove for rubbing over the crisp crumb – this is a *campesino* dish, nothing fancy. One countryman can manage the whole thing. Townies have more delicate appetites.

Eggs are the fast food of the Spanish kitchen, a legacy of the time when the population was largely rural, with a strong peasant farming tradition. When I lived in southern Spain with my young family of four children in the 1970s, although I didn't keep hens myself, I would often intercept a dozen or so from the egg lady, *la recovrera*, after she'd collected surplus supplies from our neighbours to take them for sale to the local market in Algeciras. Her suppliers would receive their payment in kind, handing over a list of household items which could not be home-produced: salt, sugar, condensed milk, coffee (a luxury, since most people brewed acorn coffee).

Although eggs found a ready market with the confectioner's of the town, vast quantities went to the sherry makers of Jerez who use the whites to refine their wine. Other uses for the whites is in the making of communion wafer; when unsanctified, the wafers are used as the basis of layer-cakes – elaborate confections made with egg-thickened confectioner's custard. The yolks left over from these activities fed a parallel industry in convent sweets, yolk-based sweetmeats (*yemas*) sold at *féria* time and on the feast days of female saints, particularly the Virgin Mary.

But it is as the housewife's stand-by – a cheap source of protein, easily stored and quickly prepared – that the egg comes into its own in the Spanish kitchen. Any housewife from La Coruña to Cadiz – at least those who can wield more than a can opener – can turn out a perfect *tortilla española* every time. A thick juicy egg-and-potato pancake which is turned in the pan (both sides must be smooth), the tortilla, with the addition of supporting ingredients that may or may not supplant the potato, has as many variations as there are days in the year. As with the bean pot, it's a statement of regional identity.

Eggs are also served *revuelto*, scrambled in olive oil with or without a small quantity of something special – wild asparagus, woodland mushrooms, or stirred into diced, cooked vegetables such as aubergine and pepper, as in the Basque *piperrada* and La Mancha's *pisto*, Spain's ratatouille. When served *al plato* – on the plate – eggs are gently fried in olive oil and set on the table in their cooking dish, a shallow earthenware *cazuela* which is heated directly on the flame. Hard-boiled eggs are also used to compensate for a shortage of meat: a vegetable stew flavoured with a ham bone can be upgraded to a main course when finished with quartered hard-boiled eggs.

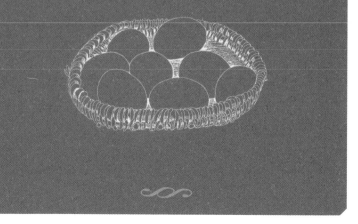

rice and pasta

paella marinera

SEAFOOD PAELLA

It's the implement which defines the dish: a shallow, double-handed raw-iron pan of Roman design. In addition, to be truly worthy of the name, the cook is always a man, preparation is in the open air and the dish is always eaten at midday, never after sundown. The same ingredients prepared by a woman in the kitchen, even if using the same implement, ingredients and method, is traditionally described as un arroz, a rice dish. The greater the pan's diameter, the more it will feed. Pans are always sold for uneven numbers of participants: 3, 5, 7 and so on. You may, however, cook it on the barbecue; the only other possible heat source is a purpose-built gas ring of a diameter suited to the pan. The key ingredients are short-grain rice, olive oil and saffron. The rest is as variable as location and seasonality dictates – always remembering that all ingredients should be uncooked when they go into the pan so that they transmit their goodness to the grains. Don't even think of lobster or anything fancy: this is field worker's food, traditionally eaten straight from the paella pan without recourse to plate or knife and fork.

Serves 6–7

**A knife tip of saffron (12–18 threads) lightly toasted in
a dry pan
4 large ripe tomatoes
6–8 tablespoons olive oil
4 garlic cloves, unpeeled and roughly chopped
1 rabbit (or 1 small chicken), jointed into
16–20 bite-sized pieces
500g short-grain rice (paella or risotto, although
pudding rice will do)
Salt and freshly milled black pepper
A handful of thin green asparagus (sprue) or young
green beans, chopped
1kg live shellfish (clams, mussels), scrubbed and beards
removed**

1 You'll need a seven-person paella pan (diameter 45cm) and a
heat source to match. To allow the rice to cook evenly in a
single layer, the pan requires an even bed of heat that allows the
full expanse of metal to come into contact with the heat source. If
this is not available, use a large frying pan and remember to stir
the rice as it cooks.

2 Put the saffron to soak in a splash of boiling water for
15 minutes or so. Meanwhile, grate the tomato flesh: cut a
tomato through the equator and empty out the seeds. Now,

holding the skin side firmly in your palm, rub the cut side through the coarse holes of the grater onto a plate. You should be left with an emptied-out shell in your hand and a juicy heap of pulp on the plate. Grate the remaining tomatoes.

3 Set the pan on the fire and wait until it is hot. Preheating the pan avoids food sticking later. Add the oil and wait until it smokes. Immediately add the garlic and the jointed rabbit (or chicken) and turn the pieces over the heat. Cook gently until tender and no longer pink, turning regularly – this will take at least 20 minutes.

4 Add the rice and stir until all the grains are coated and transparent. Stir the tomato pulp into the rice. Add the saffron and its soaking liquid and top up with as much water as will cover the layer of rice to a depth of one finger – the liquid should be level with the screws that fix the handles to the pan.

5 Allow all to bubble up, season with salt and pepper, and leave to cook for 15–18 minutes. Move the pan over the heat, and add more water when necessary, but don't stir again. After 10 minutes, add the asparagus spears or green beans and the shellfish – they'll open in the steam.

6 When it's ready, most of the liquid will have evaporated and little craters, like worm holes, will begin to appear on the surface. Test the rice for doneness by biting into a grain – it should be soft but still retain a nutty little heart.

7 Remove the pan from the heat, cover with a clean cloth or a couple of sheets of newspaper, and leave for 10 minutes to allow the rice to finish swelling. A paella should be moist and succulent, never dry.

8 Settle everyone in a circle around the pan. Traditionally you should eat the portion in front of you straight from the pan. You may use clean fingers or a spoon or lettuce leaves for scooping. Provide plenty of robust country bread for the faint-hearted who would otherwise go hungry.

NOTE: thin asparagus spears, sprue, are becoming widely available when asparagus is in season. When choosing check the cut ends for signs of drying-out and the green tips for signs of whitening. Asparagus, like cut flowers, must be absolutely fresh.

perrol de monte

MOUNTAIN RICE IN A CAULDRON

A soupy rice cooked in a two-handled copper cauldron, the perrol, with whatever the hunter brings home from the hill: partridge, pigeon, quail, wild boar, rabbit, venison and hare are all perfectly suitable. When preparing wild rabbit or hare for the pot, lift off the bluish membrane that covers the saddle and back legs, or the meat will never be tender. A perrol can also be made with tame meat – pork, chicken, beef, mutton.

Serves 8

2kg mixed game on the bone, chunked
1–2 bay leaves
½ teaspoon peppercorns
½ teaspoon allspice berries
Salt and freshly milled black pepper
1kg short-grain rice (paella or risotto rice)
Juice of 1 lemon
1 whole garlic head, separated into cloves
1 short cinnamon stick
100g serrano ham with its fat, roughly diced
1–2 links fresh chorizo or morcilla (Spanish black pudding),
cut into chunks

1 Pack the meat joints into a roomy boiling pot. Pour in enough water to submerge everything generously. Bring to the boil, skim off the grey foam that rises and add the bay leaf, peppercorns and allspice. Turn down the heat, cover loosely and simmer until the meat is perfectly tender, about 1–2 hours, depending on the age of the game.

2 Strain the broth (taste and correct the seasoning) and reserve the meat, removing the bones or not, as you please. Using a cup or a glass measure the volume of the rice. Measure out twice the volume of broth to rice. Bring the measured broth to the boil in the pot and stir in the rice.

3 Add the lemon juice, garlic cloves, cinnamon stick, serrano ham and chorizo or morcilla, and return all to the boil. Turn down the heat and cook gently for 20–30 minutes – or transfer to the oven and bake at 180°C/350°F/Gas 4 – until the broth has all been absorbed and the rice is nearly tender. Add a little more broth if necessary, the rice should remain soupy throughout.

4 To finish, remove half the rice and lay in the reserved meat on top of the rice in the pan. Top with the removed rice, and cook for another 10 minutes, until the rice is tender and the meat soft enough to eat with a spoon.

arroz abanda

TWO-DISH RICE

O ne of the two great rice dishes of the Levant – the other is the paella – for which the rice and seafood are prepared together and served separately. The fish is served first with a pungent oil and garlic sauce. Meanwhile, the rice is cooked in the broth. While the fish is variable – basically, whatever the boats have landed that day – firm-fleshed and soft-fleshed are cooked in separate batches. Among the former, most favoured are monkfish, conger eel and weever fish; among the latter, the soft-fleshed species, are mackerel, bream and gallo, a Mediterranean plaice. The heads and bones of the firm-fleshed fish are saved, along with any small crustaceans and their debris, to fortify the broth, while the heads and bones of the soft-fleshed fish are discarded, as they are bitter.

Serves 6

500g short-grain rice (paella or risotto rice)
1 thyme sprig
1 bay leaf
1 glass white wine (about 150ml)
8 tablespoons olive oil
1kg mixed fish fillets, divided into two batches, firm-fleshed
and soft-fleshed
A handful each of prawns, mussels or clams, cleaned
as appropriate
2 garlic cloves
2 tablespoons pimentón (or the pulp from 2 dried red peppers,
soaked to soften)
Salt and freshly milled black pepper
About 12 saffron threads, toasted in a dry pan
2 tablespoons chopped fresh parsley
500g tomatoes, skinned, deseeded and diced

THE ALIOLI
6 garlic cloves, peeled and crushed
1 teaspoon sea salt
About 300ml extra virgin olive oil

1 Pick over the rice, checking for little stones.

2 Bring 1.5 litres water to the boil in a roomy pan with the
herbs, wine and 4 tablespoons of oil.

3 Add the firm-fleshed fish and bring all back to the boil. Turn down the heat and leave to simmer for 5 minutes.

4 Add the soft fish and optional shellfish and crustaceans, and cook for a further 10 minutes. Carefully lift out the fish and keep it warm. Strain the fish stock and reserve.

5 Pound the garlic in a mortar with the pimentón or soaked peppers and a teaspoon of salt. Heat the remainder of the oil in a paella pan – a large frying pan will do – add the garlic and pimentón mixture, the saffron, and parsley and fry gently for a few minutes, until the garlic softens.

6 Add the rice and turn it in the hot oil for a moment. Add the tomatoes and 1 litre of fish stock – the volume of stock should be double that of the rice. Bring to the boil and let it bubble fiercely for 5 minutes, turn down the heat, and simmer for another 12 minutes. Add a little more fish stock as it dries out. Leave it to rest for 10–15 minutes after you take it off the heat. The rice should be juicy but with the grains visibly separate.

7 Meanwhile, to make the alioli, pound the garlic in a mortar with the salt. Slowly trickle in the oil, working the paste so that the garlic acts like an emulsifier to make a rich spoonable sauce for the fish.

8 Serve the sauce with the fish. By the time the fish has all been eaten, the rice will be ready. The traditional way to eat the first course is by spearing the fish on a knife straight from the communal dish. The rice, too, can be eaten directly from the pan, scooping it up with a spoon and confining yourself to the portion directly in front of you – no poaching.

> *...The paella is essentially an open-air festive dish, and, as such, falls within the masculine preserve. The paella is a pastoral dish, born under a shady tree. It is a man who must prepare it, a recognised* paellero *of good repute. It must be eaten out of the pan in which it is cooked, with the participants seated in a circle around it, each armed with his own wooden spoon....There is no doubt that the enjoyment of any dish, or indeed any beverage, inspires a particular train of thought, which in turn leads to conversation of a particular kind, in the case of the paella, rural matters: the vicissitudes of the year's weather, the price of seed-corn, recent market-prices for agricultural products, with some diversion permitted into the subject of bullfighting or the Valencian game of* pelota.

Lorenzo Millo Casas, *Discurso sobre los origines de la paella*

The rice dishes of Spain are closer in spirit to Italy's risotto – juicy, made with short-grain rice – than they are to the dry-cooked long-grain rices of the East. Saffron – sometimes reinforced with pimentón – is almost always included (although there are a few 'white' rice dishes) and the flavouring ingredients are either cooked in the broth and served first, as with *arroz a banda*, or served together with the rice, as in a paella. There are a prodigious number of variations on this basic theme: any Valencian housewife worth her paella pan can probably come up with 50 different combinations of vegetables, meat, game, fish and poultry for flavouring the basic saffron rice. Feel free to make your own contribution. Rice dishes are traditionally served only at midday. Valencians, the rice experts of Spain, maintain that anyone eating rice in the evening is either a tourist, or a native being polite to a tourist.

Pasta is not a traditional ingredient in Spanish cuisine, although small pasta shapes of the vermicelli variety are often used to fortify first-course broths. Vermicelli-type noodles – *fideos* – are also used in Catalan cooking as a replacement for rice in their regional version of the paella (a dish which takes its name from the cooking implement as well as defining the recipe itself).

moros y cristianos

LENTILS WITH RICE

The name of this dish– Moors and Christians – commemorates the epic encounter at the gates of Granada, when the Moors of Al-Andaluz were chased from their last stronghold by the combined might of Ferdinand of Aragón and Isabella of Castile. The combination – a nutrionally impeccable balance of grains and pulses – is, however, well known throughout the Middle East.

Serves 4

THE MOORS
500g lentils
Salt and freshly milled black pepper
½ large mild onion, finely chopped
2 tablespoons olive oil

THE CHRISTIANS
250g white rice, boiled and drained
1 tablespoon olive oil
2 garlic cloves, chopped

TO FINISH
2 hard-boiled eggs, quartered
2 tablespoons toasted almonds

1 Cook the lentils in enough water to cover to a depth of two fingers – they'll take 40–50 minutes to soften. Season with salt and pepper. Stir in the chopped onion and 2 tablespoons of oil. Bring back to the boil, allow one big bubble to allow the oil to form an emulsion with the lentil juices and remove from the heat and reserve.

2 Meanwhile, turn the rice and garlic in the oil in a roomy frying pan, add water to cover to a depth of two fingers. Bubble up, turn down the heat and simmer gently until tender, about 20 minutes.

3 Pile the lentils in the middle of a hot serving dish and surround with the white rice: the Moors are encircled with the Christian battalions. Finish the lentils with quartered hard-boiled eggs and the rice with the toasted almonds. Propaganda on a plate.

arroz a la cubana

CUBAN RICE

This simple but delicious combination – rice, bananas and eggs with a chilli-tomato sauce – is a re-export from Cuba, Spain's one-time colony. I loved it for my supper when I lived in Madrid as a child.

Serves 4

300g short-grain rice (paella or risotto rice)
About 4 tablespoons olive oil
Salt
500g tomatoes, skinned, deseeded and chopped
½ onion, chopped
1 garlic clove, chopped
1 tablespoon hot pimentón (Spanish chilli powder)
½ teaspoon ground allspice

TO FINISH
4 eggs (more, if people are hungry)
4 small, firm bananas, halved lengthways

1 Turn the rice in a tablespoon of oil in a heavy frying pan. Wait until the rice is transparent, then add enough water to cover all the grains completely. Allow to bubble up, then turn down the heat and cook the rice gently until tender, adding more boiling water as the grains swell. By the end of the cooking, the rice should be moist and tender but not soupy. Season with a little salt – no pepper. Transfer to a warm serving plate.

2 Meanwhile, make the sauce. Put the tomatoes, onion, garlic, pimentón or chilli and the allspice in the liquidizer with a tablespoon of oil, and process to a purée.

3 Fry the eggs sunny-side up in the remaining oil in a frying pan, and pop them onto the rice. Fry the bananas just enough to caramelize them a little – don't let them go mushy – and arrange them around the edge of the rice.

4 Reheat the frying pan and add the tomato mixture. Bubble up for a few minutes to concentrate the juices and develop the flavour – the wide surface of the pan allows this to be done fast. Hand round the sauce separately.

fideos a la catalana

PASTA PAELLA

A noodle paella, a Catalan dish in which rice is replaced by pasta of much the same volume and similar shape. Choose small elbow macaroni, spagettini broken into short lengths or the thicker varieties of soup vermicelli. As with the paella, this is a very variable recipe. Whereas pork is the usual meat, you can include prawns, shellfish, morcilla or chorizo. The almonds for the sauce, another strictly Catalan preparation, can be replaced by cubed bread.

❧

Serves 4

2 tablespoons olive oil
2 garlic cloves, chopped
2 tablespoons chopped fresh parsley
1 tablespoon blanched almonds, roughly chopped
150ml dry sherry or white wine
1 tablespoon pimentón (Spanish paprika)
1 teaspoon ground cinnamon
½ teaspoon ground cloves
12 saffron threads soaked in 1 tablespoon boiling water
250g dried pasta, such as macaroni or spaghetti
225g diced pork
1 large onion, finely chopped
Salt
500g tomatoes, skinned and chopped

1 Heat the oil in a frying pan. Fry the garlic, parsley and almonds until both are golden. Add the sherry or wine and allow to bubble up. Transfer all the solids to a food processor – or use a pestle and mortar – and process with the spices, the saffron and its soaking water until you have a smooth paste. Reserve the oil.

2 In a paella pan, or large frying pan, heat the reserved oil until a faint blue hazes rises. Add the pasta and turn it in the hot oil until it takes a little colour.

3 Add the meat and onion, sprinkle with a little salt and continue to fry until the meat and the onions lose their water and begin to caramelize.

4 Add the tomatoes and the almond paste diluted with 300ml water. Bubble up and cook gently until the meat is cooked through, the pasta is tender and the surface of the *fideu* is beginning to look dry rather than soupy. Add another splash of boiling water if it looks like drying out before the pasta is soft.

SERVING SUGGESTION: serve, if you wish to eat in traditional style, as you would a paella, unplated but with forks for everyone to eat the portion in front of them.

vegetables

habas con jamón

BROAD BEANS WITH SERRANO HAM

Young broad beans, picked while the pods are still soft and furry, are used whole for this dish. The pods have a delicate flavour rather like okra, and retain their fragrance during the cooking. If you don't use the pods, you'll need to bump up the weight. Later in the season, when the beans are already fully formed, discard the pods and make it with the beans alone. If the beans are at the end of the season and the skins are tough and leathery, slip them out of their jackets.

Serves 4

**1kg young broad beans in their pods (or 350g mature
podded beans)
4 tablespoons olive oil
1 medium onion, diced
2–3 garlic cloves, thinly sliced
2 tablespoons diced serrano ham
Small glass dry sherry or white wine (about 150ml)
Salt and freshly milled black pepper**

TO FINISH
**1 tablespoon fresh breadcrumbs
1 tablespoon chopped fresh parsley**

1 Top, tail and string the young beans in their pods, and chop them into short lengths following the swell of each bean.

2 Warm the oil in a flameproof casserole or heavy saucepan. Fry the onion and garlic for a moment without allowing them to take colour.

3 Add the beans, chopped ham, sherry or wine and enough water to cover. Add salt and freshly milled pepper, and bring all to the boil. Cover and stew gently for 1½ hours – this can be done in a gentle oven at 160°C/325°F/Gas 3. Check intermittently and add water if necessary.

4 When the beans are tender, allow to bubble up, uncovered, for a moment to evaporate the liquid – the beans should be juicy but not swimming.

5 Stir in the breadcrumbs and parsley. Reheat, taste and add more salt and pepper if necessary.

VARIATION: for a more substantial dish, scramble in one egg per person, or serve with quartered hard-boiled eggs.

pimientos fritos con ajo

FRIED GREEN PEPPERS WITH GARLIC

Frying peppers in Spain come in two kinds, both descended from the triangular Peruvian strain rather than the Mexican bell-shaped breed. The most universally available of the two (found throughout the Mediterranean) are long, thin, torpedo-shaped dark green pods with very thin flesh and a gentle, grassy flavour. The others, pimentos de Padron (named after the village in north-western Spain where they are grown) are small, short, triangular chilli-like dark green fruits with somewhat thicker flesh. Although most are mild, a few in every batch are fiery, and these are usually deep-fried to ensure they remain bright green.

Serves 4

750g green frying peppers
About 4 tablespoons olive oil
3–4 garlic cloves, unpeeled and roughly chopped
Salt

TO SERVE (OPTIONAL)
Sherry vinegar

∽♡∾

1 Rinse the peppers and shake them dry. Don't core or deseed them, leave them whole.

2 Heat the oil in a frying pan until a faint blue haze rises. Add the peppers and fry over a high heat, turning them until all sides take a little colour.

3 Turn the heat right down, add the garlic, salt lightly and cover the pan. Cook over a gentle heat until the peppers are soft, about 10 minutes.

4 Remove the lid and bubble up for a minute or two until the oil looses its moisture and begins to clear.

5 Allow to cool to room temperature and serve sauced with their own oily juices. Sprinkle with a few drops of sherry vinegar – or not, as you please.

alcachofas con habas

ARTICHOKES WITH BROAD BEANS

A classic combination from Granada's fertile market garden, the vega, known since the days of the Romans for its succulent broad beans and fine fat artichokes. It's useful to remember, when preparing the hearts, that the artichoke is a member of the daisy family and that what you're dealing with is the flower head.

Serves 4–6

8–12 artichokes (depending on size)
A squeeze of lemon juice or teaspoon vinegar
1 large onion, finely chopped
2–3 garlic cloves, finely chopped
4 tablespoons olive oil
1 glass white wine (about 150ml)
250g shelled broad beans (skinned, if old and leathery)
Salt and freshly milled black pepper
1 tablespoon chopped fresh parsley
1 tablespoon chopped fresh mint
1 tablespoon fresh breadcrumbs
1 tablespoon toasted almonds, roughly crushed

1 Prepare the artichoke hearts first: trim off the stalks close to the base. Scrape the stalks to remove the hard exterior fibres – the tender centre can be eaten – and drop into cold water with a squeeze of lemon juice or vinegar. Snap off the tough outer leaves, then, with a sharp knife, cut off the tops of the remaining leaves close to the base, exposing the small leaves which protect the choke. Nick out the inner leaves and carve out the choke. Drop the prepared hearts into the water.

2 In a roomy flameproof casserole, gently fry the onion and garlic in the oil until they soften. Add the artichoke hearts and stalks. Cover and let everything fry over a low heat for 15 minutes, shaking regularly, until the artichoke begins to take a little colour.

3 Add the wine and let it all bubble up until the liquid has reduced by half. Add the shelled beans and a glass of water. Season with salt and pepper. Allow to bubble up, turn down the heat and leave to cook gently until the vegetables are tender, about 15 minutes, adding a little boiling water if necessary.

4 Stir in the chopped parsley and mint, and a handful of breadcrumbs to thicken the juices. Finish with a sprinkle of crushed toasted almonds.

tomates rellenas con piñones

TOMATOES WITH A PINE NUT STUFFING

Pine nuts – the stone-pine's oily little seeds extracted with difficulty from their rock-hard shells – give a deliciously resiny flavour to this simple stuffing.

Serves 4

4–8 medium-sized ripe, firm tomatoes
4 tablespoons olive oil
2 garlic cloves, finely chopped
2 tablespoons pine nuts
1 tablespoon finely chopped serrano ham (optional)
1 tablespoon chopped fresh parsley
4 heaped tablespoons fresh breadcrumbs
Salt and freshly milled black pepper

1 Preheat the oven to 220°C/425°F/Gas 7. Wipe each tomato and slice a little lid off the stem end, and reserve. Scoop out the seeds and discard. Hollow out the tomatoes, reserving the pulp. Arrange the hollowed tomatoes in an oiled baking dish.

2 Warm 2 tablespoons of the oil in a small pan and fry the garlic. Add the pine nuts and let them take colour. Add the reserved tomato flesh and bubble up to make a little sauce. Stir in the ham, if using, parsley, and the breadcrumbs.

3 Stuff the tomatoes with the breadcrumb mixture. Top with the reserves lids and trickle with the remainder of the oil.

4 Bake the tomatoes for 25–30 minutes. Larger tomatoes need a slightly lower temperature and a longer cooking time. Serve at room temperature.

ensalada mixta

LETTUCE, ONION AND TOMATO SALAD

Salads of chunky raw vegetables and crisp cos lettuce leaves are preferred to soft-leaf salads – which are, in any event, too delicate to stand up to the heat of a Spanish summer.

Serves 4

1 cos lettuce, thickly sliced
1 green pepper, deseeded and finely sliced
2 large tomatoes, cut into chunks
2 small or ½ large cucumber, cut into chunks
½ mild Spanish onion, finely slivered
1–2 tablespoons green olives
Small can tuna, drained and flaked (optional)
1–2 hard-boiled eggs, peeled and quartered (optional)
6 tablespoons olive oil
2 tablespoons wine vinegar or lemon juice
Coarse sea salt

~

1 Arrange all the salad ingredients in layers on a large flat plate, finishing with the onion rings and olives. Arrange the optional extras, if using, over the top.

2 Dress with the oil, vinegar or lemon juice and a generous pinch of coarse salt – don't blend into a vinaigrette first; Spain likes the taste of its olive oil. That's all.

SERVING SUGGESTION: serve as a first course if including tuna or eggs; after the main course if not.

asadillo de pimientos

ROASTED RED PEPPERS

A classic combination of flavours and textures, this can be served as a side dish or used to sauce other vegetables – courgettes, diced aubergines, pumpkin or potato. For a more substantial dish, top with raw eggs and slip the cooking dish under the grill to set the whites – particularly good if you also include a handful of diced serrano ham.

Serves 4

2 tablespoons olive oil
4 large, juicy red peppers
2 large ripe tomatoes, thickly sliced
2 garlic cloves, sliced
1 teaspoon dried oregano

1 Preheat the oven to 230°C/450°F/Gas 8. Trickle a tablespoon of the oil into a large *cazuela* or gratin dish (or use four individual earthenware dishes).

2 Arrange the peppers and tomatoes in layers, sprinkling with the garlic slices as you go. Finish with a layer of tomato, trickle with the remaining oil and finish with the oregano. No salt or pepper is needed.

3 Bake at a high heat for 30–40 minutes, or until the juices have all evaporated and the vegetables are beginning to roast. Serve in their cooking dishes, with bread.

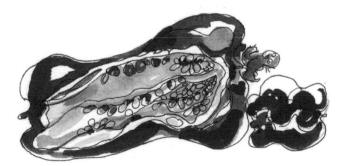

pimientos rellenos

STUFFED PEPPERS

For stuffing, you need the big, thick-fleshed, bell peppers – these can be red, yellow or green, whatever you please. The basis is rice – everything else is a matter of choice. Flavourings can be varied with diced serrano ham, mushrooms, flaked almonds or leftover chicken.

Serves 4 as a starter

4 large red peppers
2 tablespoons olive oil
2 garlic cloves, chopped
2 tablespoons toasted pine nuts
2 tablespoons raisins
1 tablespoon chopped fresh parsley
1 teaspoon cumin seeds
500g juicy tomatoes, skinned, deseeded and chopped
½ teaspoon saffron threads (about 12 threads),
soaked in a little water
250g short-grain paella or risotto rice (Calispera for choice)
Salt and freshly milled black pepper

1 Preheat the oven to 180°C/350°F/Gas 4. Wipe the peppers and cut off a lid around the stalk end, leaving the stalk in place. Empty out the seeds and pack the peppers upright, mouths pointing heavenwards, in a *cazuela* or earthenware gratin dish.

2 Heat the oil gently in a frying pan and fry the garlic until it softens a little. Add the pine nuts, raisins, parsley and cumin, and fry for a moment. Add the tomatoes and bubble up for a few minutes, mashing with a fork to soften the tomato. Add the saffron with its soaking water, and stir in the rice. Allow to bubble up then season and remove from the heat.

3 Stuff the peppers with the rice mixture, leaving plenty of room for the grains to swell. Replace the lids, cover with foil shiny side down, transfer to the oven and cook for about 1¼ hours, until the rice at the top is perfectly soft – the rice underneath will still be a little hard but will finish cooking as they cool.

4 Check after an hour and sprinkle with a little water (replace the foil) and lower the temperature if the peppers look a little dry – it all depends on the thickness of the flesh. Baste with the oily juices and serve at room temperature.

acelgas con jamón y ajo

CHARD WITH HAM AND GARLIC

*C*hard, also known as swiss chard, is a robust spinach-like vegetable with dark green leaves and pale, juicy stalks. It is popular throughout the lands of the Mediterranean in summer and winter alike. An all-year crop, in summer it's less vulnerable to heat than spinach, in winter it grows faster than cabbage (which, in any event, likes a touch of frost). The stalks and leaves are usually sold in bunches: the measurement is by volume rather than weight.

Serves 4–6

1 large bunch chard (8–12 stalks)
Salt and freshly milled black pepper
4 tablespoons olive oil
Juice and finely grated zest of 1 lemon
4 garlic cloves, finely sliced
1 tablespoon chopped serrano ham
1 tablespoon chopped fresh flat-leaf parsley

1 Rinse the chard (it grows in sandy soil and may be gritty) and separate the stalks from the leaves. Shred thickly and keep the leaves and stalks separate.

2 Cook the shredded leaves in a lidded pan with a little salt and the minimum of water until they wilt and soften, about 5 minutes or so. Drain thoroughly. Toss with half the oil, and the lemon juice and zest. Season and reserve.

3 Meanwhile, rinse the stalks and slice into lengths about as fat as your finger. Heat the remaining oil in the pan and add the garlic. Add the chopped stalks, cook for a minute, add a tablespoon of water. Bubble up, then cover tightly and cook until perfectly tender, about 10 minutes, then stir in the ham and parsley. Add pepper (no salt).

4 Serve the leaves on one side of the serving dish and the stalks on the other.

patatas en ajopollo

POTATOES WITH ALMONDS AND SAFFRON

The almond and saffron sauce, a Valencian combination, is particularly good with tender-skinned baby new potatoes. Main-crop potatoes should be peeled and cut into bite-sized chunks.

Serves 4

500g potatoes, scrubbed or peeled and cut into chunks
Salt and freshly milled black pepper
2 tablespoons olive oil
2 tablespoons blanched almonds
1 garlic clove, finely chopped
1 tablespoon fresh breadcrumbs
1 tablespoon chopped fresh parsley
12 saffron threads soaked in 1 tablespoon boiling water

1 Drop the potatoes into salted water, and set them aside.

2 Heat the oil in a small frying pan. Fry the almonds until golden, then stir in the garlic and breadcrumbs. Stir over the heat until light golden brown. Add the parsley and saffron and allow to bubble up again.

3 Tip the contents of the pan into the food processor – or use a pestle and mortar – and process with a couple of spoonfuls of water to a thick paste.

4 Drain the potatoes and transfer them to a heavy pan. Add the almond and saffron paste and pour in enough water to come halfway up the potatoes. Season. Bring to the boil, cover and cook gently until the potatoes are nearly tender, about 15 minutes, turning them halfway through the cooking to allow the top potatoes to come into contact with the heat at the bottom.

5 Remove the lid and boil rapidly until the cooking broth is reduced to a thick sauce and the potatoes are perfectly soft. Serve at room temperature.

coliflor con ajo

CAULIFLOWER WITH GARLIC

This, in my experience, is just about the only way to make cauliflower taste exotic. For a touch of luxury, stir in a handful of diced serrano ham.

∽

Serves 4

1 medium-sized cauliflower
Salt
2 tablespoons olive oil (more, if necessary)
2 garlic cloves, chopped
1 tablespoon olives, pitted and chopped
1 teaspoon cumin seeds
1 teaspoon hot pimentón (Spanish chilli powder)

1 Divide the cauliflower into bite-sized florets. Cook in boiling, salted water until tender. Drain.

2 Heat the oil in a roomy frying pan. Fry the garlic until it softens and takes a little colour.

3 Add the drained cauliflower and fry for a few minutes, or until it begins to sizzle and take a little colour.

4 Add the olives, sprinkle with cumin, season with salt and a little hot pimentón or chilli powder and fry gently for 10 minutes or so, turning the cauliflower until it browns a little and takes on the flavours of the spices. Serve at room temperature.

pisto de berejenas

BRAISED AUBERGINES

Gentle cooking enhances the sweetness of the onions which contrasts the smooth flesh and earthy flavour of the aubergines. The aubergine – known in the US as the eggplant because the varieties first planted in the gardens of Chinese immigrants to the East Coast were the small, pale-skinned egg-shaped fruits popular in Asian cooking – is one of the oldest of the Mediterranean's cultivars. Botanists identify its land of origin as India, although it's been a staple of the Iberian vegetable patch since the earliest times. Large, firm, meaty and purple-skinned in its Mediterranean incarnation, it cooks to a satisfying richness when paired, as here, with olive oil. These virtues endeared it to Spain's rural poor (as well as modern vegetarians), who called it pez de tierra, *earth-fish, and treated it as a substitute for meat.*

Serves 4

4 tablespoons olive oil
4 firm aubergines, diced
1 teaspoon cumin seeds
Salt
2 large onions, finely sliced

1 Heat half the oil in a heavy frying pan and gently fry the aubergines, sprinkled with the cumin and a little salt, until they soften and take colour: be patient – first they will soak up oil like a sponge then they will release it again, which is when they begin to fry a second time. Transfer to a sieve placed over a bowl to catch the drippings.

2 Return the drippings to the pan and fry the onions until soft and lightly golden – take your time, allow at least 20 minutes. Stir in the aubergine and cook for another 5 minutes.

3 Leave to cool to room temperature. Eat with thick slices of country bread toasted over a direct flame and rubbed with garlic. Perfect with a few slivers of manchego cheese.

berejenas fritas

FRITTERED AUBERGINES

Easy and quick: just flip and fry. Since the coating is fragile, the fritters quickly lose their crispness and are best eaten straight away. A more substantial coating which stays crisp for longer can be made by preparing an egg batter: mix 4 tablespoons (about 125g) strong bread flour with a pinch of salt and enough warm water (about 125ml) to make a thin cream; just before you're ready to fry, fold in the yolk and well-whisked white of an egg. The aubergine slices will need a preliminary dusting in flour before they're dipped in the batter and dropped in the hot oil. The same treatment can be applied to onion rings and courgettes (if small and thin, slice thickly on the diagonal to compensate for their lack of girth).

Serves 4

2 large, firm aubergines
About 150ml milk or water
4 heaped tablespoons strong bread flour
1 tablespoon semolina
1 teaspoon sea salt
Olive oil, for frying

1 Hull the aubergines and slice them into rings about as thinly as a wedding ring. Have ready the milk or water on one plate, and spread another with the flour tossed with the semolina and salt.

2 Heat a finger's depth of oil in a roomy frying pan until a faint blue haze rises.

3 Flip the slices first in the milk or water, and then dust them lightly through the flour.

4 Drop them one by one into the hot oil, only adding as many as will cover the surface of the pan. Fry until crisp and golden, turning them once. Transfer to kitchen paper to drain. Continue until all are ready, and serve piping hot.

asparagos a la parilla con salsa verde

GRILLED ASPARAGUS WITH PARSLEY SALSA

*O*nce you've tasted grilled asparagus, you'll never want to cook them any other way. The flavour comes through clear and clean and the asparagus remains juicy and lightly blistered with caramelized juices. For grilling, you need green asparagus as thick as your thumb. Cultivated asparagus is relatively new in Andalusia. Until recent times, obeying that instinct which dictates that shop-bought goods are better than fresh, canned white asparagus with bottled mayonnaise were considered a more desirable delicacy, whereas the wild-gathered spears – asparagos triguera *(wheat asparagus)* – were seen as poor man's food, fit only for including in a tortilla.

1kg green asparagus spears
Oil, for brushing

THE SALSA
4 heaped tablespoons chopped fresh flat-leaf parsley
(leaves only)
2 garlic cloves, roughly chopped
Yolk of 1 hard-boiled egg
2 tablespoons lemon juice
150ml olive oil
Salt

1 Wash and trim the asparagus, discarding the woody bits and peeling off any hard skin.

2 Preheat the grill – it needs to be good and hot.

3 Meanwhile, make the sauce: put all the ingredients except the oil in the liquidizer and purée until smooth. Add the oil in a steady trickle until the sauce thickens.

4 Arrange the asparagus on the grill pan in a single layer. Brush with oil and sprinkle with salt. Grill until they steam and blister black a little in patches, about 4 or 5 minutes in all, turning to cook all sides. Hand round the sauce separately.

Spain has an excellent choice of fine vegetables. Markets are particularly strong in the Mediterranean varieties which need plenty of sunshine: capsicum peppers, aubergines, artichokes. Tomatoes are usually of the big, juicy uneven varieties known as beef tomatoes, though in Catalonia, a special rubbing tomato – *tomate de rama* – is grown; the fruit is left on the twig and hung on a beam for storage: greenish and small, uneven in shape, it has a powerful fragrance, a remarkably viscous juice and a deliciously sweet–sour flavour, and is used for making *pan am tomaquet*, toasted bread rubbed with oil and garlic and given a finishing slick of juice.

Most of the usual northern vegetables also grow well: potatoes and carrots, leeks and onions, courgettes and cabbage. Green beans are known as *judias* (Jews) possibly because they were imports from the New World and could therefore be considered foreign. Less familiar vegetables include several varieties of wild greens, notably *tagarninas*, the leaf rosette of a large thistle and *asparagos trigeros*, wild asparagus, spindly but delicious; throughout the year, the most widely available leaf vegetable is Swiss chard, while salads are dependent on the hardy, sun-tolerant cos lettuce; winter vegetables also include cardoons, a winter-maturing member of the artichoke family – only the stalk is eaten – sold in great woolly bundles in the markets of the central plateau and the north. In the Basque country, leeks and parsley are the main event, while Galicia makes enthusiastic use of mustardy turnip greens, *grelos*.

Iberian mushroom fanciers are well-served. *Boletus* – cep or porcini mushroom – is plentiful in autumn markets, particularly in Catalonia and the Basque country, as is *Lactarius deliciosus*, saffron milk cap, a bright orange fungus which bruises blue and, when slapped on the griddle with a little chopped garlic and oil, is a favourite autumn tapa in the bars of Valencia and Barcelona. Truffles – the black Perigord rather than Italy's white Piedmont truffle – are gathered in those regions that suit their requirements, including the vicinity of Soría, which has the largest truffle-oak plantation in Europe.

fish and shellfish

pulpo encebollada con patatas

OCTOPUS WITH ONIONS AND POTATOES

*O*ctopus must be tenderized by bashing it thoroughly before you cook it – fishermen will tell you to throw it 40 times against the rocks. It's ready, they say, when the tentacles curl. Older specimens need lengthier tenderizing than young ones. Or you can make it easy for yourself and pop it in the freezer for 48 hours.

Serves 4

1 smallish octopus, about 1kg, cleaned
4 tablespoons olive oil
2 large onions, thinly sliced
1 tablespoon chopped fresh parsley
About 12 saffron threads, soaked in a little water
500g yellow-fleshed potatoes, peeled and sliced
Salt
Hot pimentón or chilli flakes

1 Rinse the octopus and slice it into bite-sized pieces.

2 Heat the oil in a roomy frying pan and fry the onions very gently until soft and golden – salt lightly to get the juices running – for 10 minutes.

3 Add the parsley and the saffron with its soaking water, and allow to bubble up.

4 Add the octopus and cook gently in its own juices – these are copious – loosely covered, for an hour. You may need to add a little water.

5 When the octopus is tender, add the potatoes, make sure there's enough liquid to cover, and continue to cook for another 15 minutes or so, until the potatoes are perfectly tender. Taste and season with salt and pimentón or chilli flakes.

6 Serve in deep bowls, sauced with its own juices.

almejas en salsa de tomate con ajo

CLAMS IN TOMATO SAUCE WITH GARLIC

A garlicky little tomato sauce into which the shellfish are dropped raw. The cooking is very brief since they only take a minute or two to open in the steam, releasing their fresh sea juices into the sauce. All bivalves can be prepared in this way.

Serves 4

2kg live shellfish – clams, mussels, cockles, razor shells, queen scallops (remove their sandy little bag of intestine and rinse well first)
½ teaspoon saffron (about 12 threads)
4 tablespoons olive oil
1 onion, finely chopped
3–4 garlic cloves, finely chopped
1kg ripe tomatoes, skinned, deseeded and diced
1 tablespoon pimentón (Spanish paprika)
1 small glass red wine (about 150ml)
Salt and freshly milled black pepper

1 Rinse the shellfish and leave them to spit out their sand in a bucket of cold water for a few hours – overnight is even better.

2 Toast the saffron in a dry pan for a minute or two until it releases its scent – don't let it burn or it will be bitter – and drop into a cup with a little boiling water. Leave to infuse for 15 minutes or so.

3 Heat the oil in a roomy frying pan and fry the chopped onion and garlic until soft and golden – don't let them brown.

4 Add the tomatoes and allow to bubble up, mashing them until they soften. Add the pimentón or paprika, the saffron with its soaking water and the wine. Bubble up again, then turn down the heat and leave to simmer for 20 minutes or so, until the sauce is thick and rich. Taste and season with salt and freshly milled black pepper.

5 Add the raw shellfish – check first to see all are looking lively. Bubble up again, turn down the heat a little, cover loosely and leave the shells to open in the steam, shaking the pan every now and again to allow the top layer to drop to the bottom. Take the pan off the heat as soon as all the shells gape open, about 4–6 minutes, depending on size of pan and thickness of shells.

calamares en su tinta

SQUID COOKED IN ITS OWN INK

A remarkably good dish, delicate and elegant: the ink that colours and flavours the sauce has a faint taste of violets, not at all fishy. Cuttlefish will do well enough instead of the squid – some say they're even better. Not everyone can handle the logistics of preparing the creatures. Fishmongers who sell them ready prepared will usually, if asked, provide a little bagful of ink. The courageous clean their own.

Serves 4

1kg whole squid, including their ink
3–4 tablespoons olive oil
4–5 garlic cloves, chopped
1 teaspoon dried thyme (or a handsome sprig of fresh)
1 teaspoon dried oregano (it dries naturally on the stalk,
just shake it in)
2–3 bay leaves
1 small red chilli, deseeded and finely chopped
A handful of celery leaves (or green celery stalks),
finely chopped
About 12 saffron threads
Salt and freshly milled black pepper
½ bottle red wine
Sugar, if necessary

1 Rinse the squid thoroughly (cephalopods are sandy creatures).

2 If preparing your own, pull the tentacled innards from the cap-like outer body, cut off the soft bits, including the eyes and the hard little beak-like mouthpiece.

3 Remove the transparent 'bone' – it looks like clear plastic – which supports the hood. Pick through the innards and rescue the silvery little ink sacks, crush them through a sieve and reserve the liquid.

4 Depending on the maturity and size, the tentacles may have little toenails embedded in their suckers which need scraping off. Slice the cap into rings and chop the tentacles – if small, leave them in their little bunch. Rinse your hands in cold water and they won't smell fishy.

5 Warm the oil in a roomy saucepan and add the garlic. When it begins to sizzle, add the prepared squid. Turn up the heat, and stir until the flesh stiffens and turns opaque.

6 Add the herbs, chilli, celery leaves and saffron and a generous amount of freshly milled pepper. Pour in the wine, bring to the boil, turn down the heat, cover loosely and leave to simmer gently for about 40 minutes, or until the flesh is perfectly tender and the juices well-reduced.

7 Stir in the reserved ink, taste and season – perhaps add a little sugar if the wine was a bit rough. Serve immediately.

sepia con habas

CUTTLEFISH WITH BROAD BEANS

The creamy chewiness of the fish marries perfectly with the tender greenness of the beans. Squid can be substituted for the cuttlefish, and white beans, the large, floury pochas or the smaller kidney-shaped habichuelas, can replace the broad beans.

Serves 4–6

1kg whole squid or cuttlefish
2 tablespoons olive oil
2 garlic cloves, finely sliced
250g shelled, skinned broad beans (fava)
1 wine glass dry sherry (about 150ml)
1 teaspoon fresh marjoram or oregano leaves
Salt and freshly milled black pepper

1 Rinse the fish, remove the bone and the soft innards with the tentacles and body attached. Discard the innards and the eye portion as well as the hard little mouthpiece: a beaky protuberance. Slice the body and remaining head parts into rings. Rinse the tentacles and scrape off the little toenails. If large, divide the tentacles into singles; if small, the tentacles look pretty left in their bunches.

2 Heat the oil gently in a flameproof casserole. Add the garlic and let it soften but not take colour. Add the fish and let it cook very gently until it yields up its juices, about 10 minutes.

3 Add the beans, the sherry and the same volume of water (about 150ml) and let it all bubble up. Sprinkle in the oregano or marjoram, season with pepper, turn down the heat, cover loosely and leave to simmer for 20–30 minutes, or until the beans and the fish are tender.

4 Remove the lid, turn up the heat and bubble up to reduce the juices to an oily sauce. Taste and add salt. Serve with chunks of robust bread for mopping.

zarzuela catalana

CATALAN FISH SOUP

The Catalan version of Provence's bouillabaisse, a member of that venerable tribe of Mediterranean fish soups which makes the most of whatever comes to hand. The creatures that were too small or strange or bony to find a market, the zarzuela or ragbag left at the end of the day, went into the fishwife's soup pot. Since the result was more delicious than anything the paying customers put on the table, these one-pot stews remain popular, their content becoming grander all the time.

Serves 4 as a main dish

500g monkfish tail, filleted
500g sea bream, filleted
350g squid cleaned
500g raw mussels in the shell
Salt and freshly milled black pepper
2–3 tablespoons plain flour
100ml olive oil
1 small onion, finely sliced
2 garlic cloves, finely slivered
500g ripe tomatoes, skinned, deseeded and diced
1 short length cinnamon stick
About 12 saffron threads, toasted in a dry pan
1 small glass dry sherry or white wine (about 150ml)
12 large raw prawns or langoustines
2 tablespoons chopped fresh parsley

∞

1 Chop the fish fillets into bite-sized pieces and slice the squid into rings, leaving the tentacles in a bunch. Set aside. Scrape the mussels and remove their sandy little beards. Discard any that do not close when sharply tapped. Put them in a roomy flameproof pot with 500ml lightly salted water. Bring to the boil, cover and cook for 5 minutes or so, until the shells open.

2 Remove the pot from the heat and transfer the mussels with a draining spoon to a warm serving dish. Discard any that remain closed. Strain the broth through a cloth-lined sieve – mussels are hard to rid of all their sand – and reserve.

3 Dust the fish pieces through a plateful of seasoned flour.

4 Heat the oil in a roomy frying pan. Fry the floured fish for 2–3 minutes on each side, until firm and golden. Transfer to the serving dish with the mussels.

5 Reheat the pan and gently fry the onion and garlic until they soften – don't let them brown.

6 Add the tomatoes, cinnamon and saffron, and bubble up for a few minutes until the tomato softens, mashing down to make a thick sauce.

7 Add the dry sherry or white wine and bubble up to evaporate the alcohol.

8 Add the mussel broth and bubble up, stirring to blend. Taste and season with pepper – you probably won't need more salt.

9 Lay the prawns or langoustines in the hot broth. Allow to bubble up, and cook briefly until they turn opaque. Transfer the prawns to the serving dish. Bubble up the sauce again until thick and rich. Ladle the sauce over the fish and finish with a generous shower of parsley.

> *Between the hand and the mouth the soup is lost.*
> **Spanish saying**

bacalao a la brasa con salsa romesco

GRILLED SALT COD WITH RED PEPPER AND ALMOND SALSA

The salty chewiness of the fish is perfectly balanced by the sweetness and richness of the salsa, a speciality of the Catalan city of Tarragona. The deep red of the sauce comes from roasting the tomatoes as well as the peppers, ñoras, which need to be soaked and scraped from the skin.

Serves 4–6

250g salt cod, soaked for 48 hours in several changes of water

THE SALSA ROMESCO
2 dried red peppers, deseeded and soaked to swell
2 large ripe tomatoes, cut into chunks
2 garlic cloves, crushed
1 teaspoon salt
2 tablespoons fresh breadcrumbs fried crisp in a little olive oil
2 tablespoons toasted almonds
1 dried red chilli, deseeded and crumbled
2 tablespoons red wine vinegar
150ml olive oil

1 Drain the fish and remove the bones and skin – feel carefully with your fingers. Grill fiercely until the flesh blisters and blackens a little at the edges. Shred into small pieces.

2 Roast the peppers and tomatoes under the grill until they blister and take colour. Scrape the pulp from the skin of the peppers, skin the tomatoes, scooping out and discarding the seeds, and drop them in the liquidizer with the garlic, salt, breadcrumbs and almonds. Pulverize to a paste (or use a pestle and mortar).

3 Add the crumbled red chilli and the wine vinegar. Add the oil in a thin trickle, as for a mayonnaise, and process until the sauce is thick and shiny. Fold the shredded salt cod with the salsa and serve with bitter leaves, such as frizzy endive or chicory.

NOTE: if you can't find dried red peppers, *ñoras*, replace with 2 tablespoons pimentón (Spanish paprika).

pez espada a la plancha con alioli

SWORDFISH STEAKS WITH GARLIC SAUCE

Swordfish and tuna, migratory fish which pass from the wide Atlantic through the Straits of Gibraltar to spawn in the Mediterranean, are treated more like steak than fish, and are often served as the main course in a meal. The flavour is robust enough to stand up to an alioli – a garlicky mayonnaise made without eggs. Although traditionally made in a pestle and mortar, it works well in the liquidizer. For a thicker, more mayonnaise-like sauce, include a whole egg.

Serves 4

4 swordfish steaks, each about 150g apiece
Salt and freshly milled black pepper
1 tablespoon olive oil

THE ALIOLI
4 large garlic cloves
1 tablespoon fresh white breadcrumbs
Juice of 1 lemon
½ teaspoon salt
300ml olive oil

1 Set the fish to soak for 20 minutes in cold salted water to firm the flesh and drain out any blood.

2 Meanwhile, make the alioli. Put the garlic cloves, breadcrumbs, lemon juice and salt in a liquidizer or food processor and blend to a thick paste. Add the oil in a thin stream until the sauce forms an emulsion and thickens.

3 Drain the fish steaks and pat dry. Rub the cut surfaces with oil, and season with salt and pepper.

4 Heat a griddle or heavy iron frying pan until it is smoking hot. Smack on the swordfish steaks. Grill them fast for 2–3 minutes each side, turning once. Serve the fish with the sauce on the side.

NOTE: An alioli can be served with fried fish, or plain cooked vegetables – in fact, whenever and wherever a garlicky mayonnaise would be appropriate. You can also stir it into a fish soup, to add texture and richness and flavour.

besugo al horno con patatas

SEA BREAM BAKED WITH POTATOES

A simple way with a fresh fish, and one which makes an expensive luxury go further. The potatoes take the flavour of the fish, and the tomatoes and onions melt to make a rich sauce with the oil.

Serves 4

1 sea bream (about 1.5kg), gutted and scaled but with the head left on
Coarse sea salt
1–2 bay leaves
1 lemon, quartered
500g potatoes, peeled and cut into bite-sized pieces
500g onions, quartered
500g firm tomatoes, cut into chunks
500g green peppers, deseeded and cut into chunks
1 wine glass dry white wine (about 150ml)
4 tablespoons olive oil

1 Preheat the oven to 180°C/350°F/Gas 4. Wipe over the fish and salt it lightly inside and out. Tuck the bay leaves and lemon quarters into the cavity. Set aside at room temperature.

2 Arrange the vegetables in a roasting tin, pour in the wine, trickle with the oil and cover with foil, shiny side down. Bake for 30 minutes or so, until the potatoes are tender.

3 Remove the foil. Place the fish on the bed of vegetables, replace the foil and bake for another 10 minutes, until the fish is cooked right through. It's ready when the thickest part feels firm to your finger.

4 Remove and leave to rest for another 10 minutes to allow the heat to reach right through to the bone.

bacalao ajo arriero

MULE-DRIVER'S SALT COD

A dish for travellers – mule-drivers – since salt fish can be carried in the pocket and reconstituted at will. However, the saltiness of the fish, the sweetness of the garlic and the punch of the hot chillies is so good that the dish continued to be prepared long after the need for it had gone. Choose middle-cut salt cod with a clean, creamy colour and no sign of pink along the bone. If the fish looks very white, take it as a sign it's been artificially bleached.

Serves 4

250g salt cod
150ml olive oil
4 red peppers, deseeded and cut into ribbons
1 whole garlic head, separated into cloves
2–3 dried chillies, deseeded and finely chopped
1 tablespoon black olives

1 Soak the fish for a day and a night in several changes of water – allow no more than 18 hours, or it will lose its flavour.

2 Skin, bone and flake the fish into small pieces – use your fingers. If it's still too tough to flake, simmer in water for 5 minutes first.

3 Heat 4 tablespoons of the oil in a heavy frying pan and fry the pepper ribbons and the garlic cloves (peeled or not, as you please) until the garlic softens and becomes golden (don't let it burn) and the peppers are a little caramelized. Be patient – it will take 15–20 minutes. Remove and reserve.

4 Wipe the pan to remove all but a fine coating of oil, and reheat until smoking. Drop the cod flakes into the pan and fry fiercely until the edges curl and crisp a little, about 3–4 minutes will do the trick.

5 Toss the fish and vegetables together and finish with a sprinkle of chilli and a fistful of olives. Serve at room temperature.

SERVING SUGGESTION: this is nice piled on thick slabs of toasted country bread (you can pop the slices in the pan for a lovely roasted flavour). For a more substantial dish, serve with quartered hard-boiled eggs.

marmitakua

TUNA AND POTATO CASSEROLE

A one-pot dish, simple and good, which takes its name from the cooking pot, the marmita, a heavy iron pot used to prepare supper by Basque fishermen on their long sea voyages. The dish, understandably considering its history, is now the speciality of the Sociedades Gastronomicas, land-based cooking clubs originally established by sailors nostalgic for the cameraderie of life at sea. These days, although women are admitted under sufferance, the clubs provide an outlet for husbands and fathers who love to cook but are obliged (or prefer) to leave the domestic kitchen to their women. The ingredients can vary – garlic and peppers may be omitted – but the method is always the same.

Serves 4

1kg fresh tuna, diced into bite-sized pieces
1 wine glass olive oil (about 150ml)
2 mild red onions, finely sliced
2 garlic cloves, finely sliced
2 large ripe tomatoes, skinned and chopped
2 green peppers, deseeded and diced
1 level tablespoon pimentón (Spanish paprika)
1kg yellow-fleshed potatoes, peeled and cut into
bite-sized chunks
Salt and freshly milled black pepper

TO SERVE
4 thick slices country bread

1 Salt the tuna pieces and set aside.

2 Heat the oil in a flameproof pot and add the chopped onions. Let them sizzle gently until softened and golden – don't let them burn.

3 Add the garlic, tomatoes, peppers and pimentón (or paprika), and bubble up. Add the potatoes, turn them in the oily juices, and add just enough cold water to submerge everything in the

pan. Bring slowly to the boil and cook, loosely covered, until the potatoes are tender but still hold their shape, about 20 minutes.

4 Add the tuna, allow to bubble up – allow one big belch – then turn down the heat. Cover loosely and cook for a further 5–6 minutes – no more or the fish will toughen. Season with salt and pepper.

5 Serve in deep soup plates, with thick slabs of home-made bread. The bread may be placed in the plate and the soup ladled over the top, or it can serve as a mop for the remains of the broth.

NOTE: Spanish cooks prefer the long-fin tuna, *bonito blanco*, a large tuna caught off the Cantabrian coast in the summer months. Its firm, pale, almost creamy-coloured flesh has a delicate flavour likened to milk-fed veal.

⁓

While the pale-fleshed long-fin tuna caught in the Bay of Biscay is usually eaten fresh, the canners and salters of Valencia and Huelva prefer the larger, ruby-fleshed blue-fin tuna traditionally trapped on migration from the cold waters of the Atlantic to its breeding grounds in the eastern Mediterranean. The catch (these days, mostly imported from Pacific waters) is either brined and conserved under oil as *atun en conserva*, a popular quick tapa; or dry-salted and wind-dried as *mojama*, the fishy equivalent of serrano ham, one of the great luxuries of the Spanish table. In the old days, conserved tuna was sold by weight from the barrel, though nowadays it comes in cans; either way, it's good with a little chopped onion, or crushed into the yolk of a hard-boiled egg. *Mojama* is eaten very finely sliced and dressed with a little olive oil, though the most prized cut, *ventreja* – buttery, tender belly-meat – needs no such attention. *Botargo de atún*, the salt-cured, wind-dried roe, is sold at caviar prices: delicious grated over a seafood paella, or slivered onto toasted country bread rubbed with olive oil and garlic.

atún en escabeche

HOT-PICKLED TUNA

The tuna takes particularly well to a spice bath, a valuable method of preservation in pre-refrigeration days. For those who lived in the uplands well back from the long sea coast and had limited access to fresh fish, it was not only useful, it also added variety to the diet. Mackerel, usually the cheapest fish on the slab, also takes happily to the treatment.

Serves 4

4 thick tuna steaks, about 1kg
Salt
1 heaped tablespoon flour
1 tablespoon pimentón (Spanish paprika)
2 tablespoons olive oil
1 medium onion, finely sliced
1 garlic clove, crushed
1 small carrot, sliced
1 tablespoon chopped fresh parsley
1 bay leaf, torn
6 peppercorns, roughly crushed
1 teaspoon crumbled dried oregano
4 tablespoons sherry vinegar (or any other good vinegar)

1 Sprinkle the tuna steaks with salt and leave to firm and juice for 30 minutes. Pour off any liquid, pat the fish dry and dust each steak lightly through the flour mixed with the pimentón or paprika.

2 Heat a frying pan and add a tablespoon of oil. Lay the fish in the hot oil and fry for 2–3 minutes, or until the flesh is opaque and the exterior a little browned – take care not to overcook. Transfer to a shallow dish in a single layer.

3 Reheat the pan, add the remaining oil and gently fry the onion for a few minutes until soft – don't let it brown.

4 Add the remaining ingredients and bubble up to blend the flavours and soften the carrot. Pour this warm scented bath, unstrained, over the fish. Cover with a clean cloth and leave overnight in a cool place.

5 Spoon the pickle over the fish whenever you remember. Ready to eat in a day, better in two, best in three.

empanadillas de atún

TUNA TURNOVERS

An empanadilla *is a turnover similar a pasty: portable and convenient. The yeast-raised dough can be replaced with a shortcrust pastry made with lard – a hot water crust is perfect. Individual turnovers are* empanadillas; *the* empanada, *which is more common, is the family version baked in a large rectangular tin and sold in bakeries by weight, cut into squares. Recipes vary: some people leave out the tomatoes, others the parsley, some include garlic rather than onion. Salmon, once plentiful in the rivers of northern Spain, can take the place of tuna.*

Serves 6–8

500g tuna steaks, diced
Salt
1 red pepper, deseeded and diced
1 large potato, peeled and diced
½ onion, diced small
1 large tomato, skinned, deseeded and diced
1 teaspoon dried thyme
Pinch of chilli powder
1 glass white wine (about 150ml)

THE PASTRY
275g strong bread flour
½ teaspoon salt
25g fresh yeast (12g dried)
50g fresh pork lard or olive oil
2 tablespoons white wine
Egg yolk, for glazing
Oil, for brushing

1 Salt the tuna and set aside to firm and drain while you make the dough.

2 To make the pastry, sift the flour with the salt into a warm bowl. Crumble in the yeast if fresh, or mix it in if using dried or easy-blend.

3 Put the lard or oil into a small pan with the wine and 150ml water and heat it to blood temperature.

4 Work the warm liquid into the flour and knead it with the ball of your hand until you have a smooth, springy dough. Cover with clingfilm and leave to rise in a warm place for an hour or so, until doubled in size.

5 Meanwhile, prepare the filling. Heat the oil in a roomy frying pan and fry the onion, diced pepper and potato until soft and golden.

6 Add the tomato, season with thyme, salt and a pinch of chilli, and allow to bubble up. Add the wine, bubble up again until the alcohol evaporates, then remove from the heat and fold in the diced tuna. Reserve while you finish the dough.

7 Cut the dough into 20 pieces. Roll out each piece between two sheets of clingfilm to give you a fist-sized round of dough. Spread half the round with the filling, leaving a margin around the edge, dampen the edges and fold the top over the filling to enclose. Continue until the filling and dough is all finished.

8 Prick the tops and brush with a little beaten egg. Transfer to an oiled baking tray and leave to rise again for another 30 minutes in a warm place.

9 Preheat the oven to 190°C/375°F/Gas 5. Bake the pasties for 10–15 minutes, depending on the thickness of the pastry, until risen and well browned. Transfer to a wire rack to cool. Serve at room temperature.

NOTE: to skin tomatoes, make a small cross in the skin and place in a heatproof bowl of boiling water for about 10 seconds. Drain and immerse them in another bowl of cold water to cool a little. Using the tip of a sharp knife, peel off the skin beginning at the cross.

guiso de pescado

FISH HOTPOT

Homely but classic, this is a fish stew which has no need of fancy sauces. Ask the fishmonger for the heads and bones to make a stock. Salt-cured cod, bacalao, *can be used instead of fresh fish: soak for 48 hours in several changes of water.*

❧

Serves 4

lkg white fish fillets
Salt
150ml olive oil
2 large onions, sliced
3–4 garlic cloves, sliced
1 tablespoon chopped serrano ham
1 litre fish stock (made with heads and bones)
300ml white wine
1 bay leaf
1kg yellow-fleshed potatoes, peeled and sliced lengthways
500g chard or spinach, roughly shredded

1 Skin the fish fillets if necessary and remove any whiskery bones. Chop into bite-sized pieces. Salt lightly and set aside.

2 Heat the oil gently in a roomy saucepan. Add the onions and garlic, salt lightly and fry very gently for 20 minutes or so, until soft and golden – don't let them brown.

3 Add the serrano ham and the stock, wine and bay leaf, and boil rapidly until the volume is reduced by half.

4 Add the potatoes and simmer gently for 15–20 minutes, until just tender. Add the shredded chard or spinach and bubble up until the leaves wilt.

5 Lay in the fish, return the broth to the boil and cook for another 4–5 minutes – just long enough for the fish to turn opaque. Serve in deep bowls and eat with a spoon and fork.

Spain harvests magnificent seafood from its long coastlines, both Atlantic and Mediterranean. Most of this bounty is marketed fresh and unprocessed, trucked through the night to ensure the inland cities – Madrid and the cities of the plain – get their fish as soon as possible after it's caught. So wide is the variety that the vocabulary to describe the different sea creatures changes from coast to coast and even port to port. When choosing seafood in a bar, the eye and the finger are often the only communication possible to all but the native born. To make this easy, sea delicacies are usually laid out for the customers' inspection on a cold counter, priced by weight and cooked to order.

Lobster and prawns are the ultimate luxury, often imported from elsewhere, fetching prices to match. Less familiar native sea creatures include sea tomatoes, sea lemons, sea dates, sea urchins, spike-shelled sea snails, spider crabs, swimmers, shore crabs, and, most esteemed of all, the percebe or goose-necked barnacle, a cliff-clinger which lives in colonies, looks like a bunch of miniature elephant's feet and tastes like lobster. Add to that a basketful of familiar bivalves – mussels, oysters, clams, razor shells, scallops, cockles – and it's easy to see why so many of Spain's best eating emporiums specialize in seafood.

The larger fish – particularly steak fish such as swordfish and tuna, which fetch a higher price and have a relatively long shelf life – are the most suitable for shipping off elsewhere. Smaller varieties, and those of less gastronomic worth, are more likely to stay close to home, as candidates for the housewife's frying pan. Among fish friers, there are none better than the Andalusian: if the cooks of Andalusia could capture the sea foam, the saying goes, they'd fry it to perfection. As it is, they do well enough with cuttlefish, squid, sardines, anchovies and such oddities as sea anemones and sand shrimp. Also enjoyed are the sweet-fleshed little flat fish that make their home on the tide flats, *chunquetes* – tiny fish-fry with pinhead eyes, although these are no longer legally tradeable. Most delicious of all, the beautiful red mullet with its bright, dark eyes and gilded scales, for which, when fresh, no price is considered too high.

beans and pulses

habas con castañas

BROAD BEANS WITH CHESTNUTS

The chestnut and the broad or fava bean were the storecupboard staples of Mediterranean Europe until the arrival of the New World's easy-grow crops: maize, haricot beans and potatoes. In the sierras along the Portuguese border, pig country, which is a land of extremes, where the summers are blazing and the winters icy, the chestnut is still used as fodder for man and beast. In this dish from the sierras of Seville, dried favas are combined with dried chestnuts. The finishing flavouring of cilantro, fresh coriander leaves, is found nowhere else in Spain, a result of trade with the pig herdsmen of Portugal, who acquired the taste from trade with the Orient.

Serves 6–8

350g dried skinned broad beans, soaked overnight
1 short length serrano ham bone or a bacon knuckle
1 chicken quarter
350g dried chestnuts, soaked overnight (or 500g
fresh ones, skinned)
2 tablespoons olive oil
1 onion, roughly chopped
1 large carrot, chopped
1 bay leaf
1 thyme sprig
$\frac{1}{2}$ teaspoon crushed black peppercorns
1 short length cinnamon stick
Salt

TO FINISH
About 250g pumpkin, deseeded, peeled and diced
About 2 tablespoons chopped fresh coriander
1–2 links fresh (soft) chorizo, crumbled and fried (optional)

1 Drain the beans and put them in a roomy, flameproof stewpot
with the ham bone or bacon knuckle and the chicken quarter.
Add enough water to cover all to a depth of two fingers. Bring to
the boil and skim off any grey foam that rises.

2 Add the remaining ingredients and return to the boil. Turn
down the heat, cover loosely and leave to bubble gently for
1–1½ hours, or until the beans and chestnuts are perfectly soft.
Add the diced pumpkin. Return to the boil and bubble up for
15 minutes or so, until the pumpkin is perfectly tender. Taste
and adjust the seasoning if necessary and finish with a generous
handful of chopped coriander.

3 Serve in deep soup plates, with rough red wine for the
digestion and bread for mopping. Finish, if you like, with
crumbled fresh chorizo fried in its own oily juices.

puchero andaluz

CHICKPEA AND CHICKEN STEW

Spain's pucheros *and* cocidos – *the generic names for anything that combines pulse vegetables with a scrap of meat or bones and is cooked in a boiling pot – have their origin in Moorish Andalusia, although the dish is now naturalized throughout the land. Each region has its own particular recipe, although these can change from household to household, with ingredients added or subtracted according to preference, purse and available raw materials. Here's how they like it in Andalusia, where I cut my culinary teeth. My children called these dishes beans-and-bones, and insist I cook them when we gather together for a family party.*

Serves 4–6

500g chickpeas, soaked overnight
½ head garlic
Short length ham bone or bacon knuckle
2 chicken quarters (a boiling fowl is best, a chicken will do)
1 bay leaf
½ teaspoon coriander seeds
6–8 black peppercorns
1 onion, roughly chopped
1 bay leaf and a majoram sprig
Salt

TO FINISH

1–2 large potatoes, peeled and cut into bite-sized pieces
Generous handful of spinach or chard leaves, shredded
2 tablespoons olive oil

1 Drain the chickpeas and put them into a pan of water. Bring all to the boil. Skim off the grey foam.

2 Hold the clump of garlic in a flame until the papery covering blackens at the edges, and the air is filled with the fine scent of roasting garlic cloves. Drop it into the pot with the ham bone or bacon knuckle, chicken quarters, bay leaf, coriander seeds and peppercorns. Add the onion and herbs. No salt.

191

3 Bring to the boil and turn down the heat. Cover and cook for 1½–3 hours, or until the chickpeas are quite soft.

4 Keep the soup at a gentle boil – don't let the temperature drop or add salt; if you do the chickpeas never seem to soften. If you need to add water, make sure it is boiling. Thirty minutes before the end of cooking, add the potatoes.

5 Ten minutes before the end, stir in the spinach or chard. Just before you are ready to serve, add salt and stir in the oil.

SERVING SUGGESTION: serve in deep plates with plenty of bread and a cos lettuce and onion salad on the side.

The original bean of the Old World was the fava (broad bean) in its dried and storable state. The fava was replaced after 1492 with the New World's haricots, although not before it had given its name to one of the most famous of Spain's many bean dishes, the Asturian *fabada*. Which is not to say that there's any one recipe that can be called authentic, or even that fava beans are to be found therein (times change): there are simple *fabadas* and luxurious *fabadas*, *fabadas* made with a dozen different meats, and those made with just the bare essentials. Asturians claim that the cassoulet of France is no more than a *fabada asturiana* from the wrong side of the Pyrenees that has taken itself too seriously.

The fava was not alone in the pre-Columbian storecupboard. Chickpeas, dried chestnuts and brown lentils provided the bulk of Spain's medieval diet. Bean dishes – one-pot soup-stews, although often served as two or even three courses – continue to provide the working population with a perfectly-balanced meal each and every day of the year. No region of Spain (or, for that matter, Portugal) is without its particular combination of beans and bones, although all include some form of embutido – preserved pork product – with the rest dictated by season, purse and local preference. In Andalusia and the Levant, chickpeas are popular. In the north, the big flat creamy lima bean – also called butter bean – is preferred. The Madrid bean pot is the most luxurious, including beef and a good selection of everyone else's ingredients as well as its own. Leftover caldo, broth, from the beanpot is saved to make croquetas (croquettes, see page 34), or to provide the basis for a first-course soup.

garbanzos con callos

CHICKPEAS WITH CHILLI AND TRIPE

The soft, gluey texture of tripe – you love it or hate it – combines particularly well with chickpeas and chilli. The dish is also known as callos a la madrileña, a favourite of the capital's tapa bars. Offal dishes are generally for townies rather than country people since the raw materials, off-cuts of the butcher's trade, are easily available in cities that have their own slaughterhouses. You will find them in all ship-victualling ports – particularly those that supplied the trans-atlantic trade – Seville and Cadiz.

Serves 4–6

500g chickpeas, soaked overnight
500g prepared tripe, cubed or cut into narrow ribbons
1 tablespoon diced serrano ham or short length ham bone
2 garlic cloves, crushed
2 bay leaves
125g chorizo
½ teaspoon black peppercorns, crushed

TO FINISH
4 tablespoons olive oil
2 garlic cloves, crushed
1 red pepper, deseeded and chopped
500g tomatoes, skinned and chopped (or canned)
6–8 small chillies, fresh or dried, deseeded and finely chopped
1 small glass red wine (about 150ml)
Salt

1 Drain the chickpeas and put them in a roomy, flameproof pot with the tripe, ham or ham bone, garlic, bay leaves, chorizo, peppercorns and enough water to cover everything to a depth of two fingers.

2 Bring to the boil, skim off any grey foam that rises and turn down the heat a little – chickpeas should never come off the boil. Leave to bubble gently, loosely covered, for 1½–2 hours, or until the chickpeas are perfectly tender and have absorbed most of the cooking broth. If you need to add water, make sure it's boiling before you add it.

3 Meanwhile, make the finishing sauce: heat the oil in a frying pan, and gently fry the garlic and pepper until they are softened and golden.

4 Add the tomatoes, chillies and wine, and allow to bubble up. Turn down the heat and leave to simmer for 20–25 minutes, or until thick and jammy.

5 Stir this sauce into the stew as soon as the chickpeas are perfectly soft, and continue to cook gently for 10–15 minutes to marry the flavours. Taste and add salt and a little more chilli if that's what it needs – pepperiness does wonders for tripe.

197

olla podrida

BEAN POT WITH CHORIZO, CHICKEN AND BEEF

This is the stupendous bean pot as served in Madrid (also known as cocido madrileño), which is as splendidly extravagant as can be expected from the nation's political capital, and is just as variable in its notions of what's acceptable. Although chickpeas are traditionally the basis, the version prepared by my mother's cook when I lived in Madrid as a teenager in the 1950s was based on white haricot beans, habichuelas, an ingredient she considered more digestible and modern. The dish was always served at midday and only in the cold months. In the autumn, sweet potato and apples were included, in the winter there was quince.

Serves 6–8

750g haricot beans, soaked overnight
½ garlic head (about 6 cloves)
1 short length serrano ham bone or bacon knuckle
4 tablespoons olive oil
1–2 bay leaves
2 dried red peppers, deseeded and torn or 1 fresh red pepper,
deseeded and sliced
½ teaspoon peppercorns, crushed
1 small chicken (an old hen has the best flavour, a
young one will do)
750g stewing beef in a single piece (shin, for preference)
500g pork belly, salted or fresh
1–2 large carrots, cut into chunks
1 onion stuck with 2–3 cloves
Salt and freshly milled black pepper

TOMATO SAUCE
1 onion, diced
2 tablespoons olive oil
1kg ripe tomatoes, skinned and chopped

TO FINISH
250g chorizo
250g morcilla or black pudding
1 large sweet potato, peeled and cut into chunks
1 small green cabbage
2 green apples, peeled, cored and chunked
1 tablespoon olive oil

1 Drain the beans, put them in a heavy saucepan and pour in enough cold water to submerge them to a depth of two fingers. Bring to the boil and skim off the grey foam that rises.

2 Meanwhile, spear the garlic on a knife and hold the whole thing in a flame to char the paper covering and roast the cloves a little. Drop them into the bean pot along with the ham bone or bacon knuckle, oil, bay leaves, peppers and peppercorns. Bring all to the boil, and then turn down to a fast simmer. Cover loosely and leave to bubble gently, adding boiling water during the course of the cooking when needed. Beans are variable in the length of time they need to soften and can take anything from 1–3 hours to cook.

3 Meanwhile, put the chicken, beef and pork in another pan with the carrots and the onion stuck with the cloves, and add enough water to submerge all completely. Season with salt and pepper. Bring to the boil, skim and turn down the heat. Cover loosely and leave to simmer until all is tender.

4 In a small saucepan, make the tomato sauce: fry the onion in the oil gently until it softens and browns a little, then add the tomatoes. Allow to bubble up and then squash down with a fork until you have a thick, shiny deep-red sauce. Season and reserve.

5 When the haricot beans are soft but not yet mushy, add the chorizo, black pudding and sweet potato. Bubble up again and turn down the heat to a simmer. Test for doneness after 20 minutes.

6 Meanwhile, prepare the cabbage: with a sharp knife, nick out the hard centre of the core, then slice thickly, making sure

each slice is held together by a strip of stalk. Pack the cabbage slices in a roomy saucepan and add a couple of ladlesful of broth from the meats. Bring to the boil, drop in the apples. Cover tightly and cook until tender but still bright green, about 5 minutes.

7 To finish, taste and add salt (if you have used salt pork it will have contributed to the saltiness), and stir in an extra spoonful of oil. Remove the chorizo and morcilla from the bean pot and heap them on a serving dish with the meats from the other pot. Moisten with cooking broth. Heap the meats, vegetables and beans in separate piles on another serving plate.

8 Serve the bean broth combined with the meat broth first in deep plates in which you may, if you wish, place a slice of toasted bread rubbed with garlic, and serve the real food – beans, meats and vegetables including the cabbage and apples – as a second course. Serve the tomato sauce separately.

fabada asturiana

BUTTER BEANS WITH PORK

The Asturians – dairy-herding upland farmers with a tradition of self-sufficiency – prefer the Peruvian native bean, the lima, butter bean – a large, flattish ivory-coloured bean – to the other storable beans, all of which are descended from the rounder, smaller Mexican brown bean. Not only does the lima thrive in the cold climate of the highest mountain range in Spain but it melts to a comforting creaminess in a stew.

Serves 6–8

750g smallish butter beans, soaked overnight
½ garlic head
1 large carrots, diced
2 small turnips, peeled and diced
2 celery sticks, diced
500g pork spare rib
250g chorizo
250g morcilla or black pudding (optional)
Sea salt and freshly milled black pepper

1 Drain the beans and rinse them. Put them in the soup pot with the rest of the ingredients and enough water to cover them to a depth of two fingers. No salt yet.

2 Bring to the boil and turn down to simmer. Cover loosely and leave to bubble gently for 1–2 hours, or until the beans are perfectly soft and the meats tender enough to eat with a spoon.

SERVING SUGGESTION: serve in deep soup plates. If you like, hand a bowl of chopped parsley and raw onion for people to add their own.

habas verdes con longaniza y gachas de maîz

FLAGEOLETS WITH CHORIZO AND CORNMEAL CRUMBS

*I*n northern Spain, the dried green beans the French call *flageolets – dried haricots picked green – are esteemed for their delicate flavour and slightly gluey texture. In this dish from Catalonia, they're combined with the long thin lightly smoked chorizo known as* longaniza, *and served with crisp fingers of cornmeal porridge.*

Serves 4–6

350g green flageolet beans, soaked for 2–3 hours
100g serrano ham or lean bacon, diced
2–3 garlic cloves, peeled
1 bay leaf
1 small thyme sprig
½ teaspoon peppercorns, crushed

1 *longaniza* or 150g soft chorizo, sliced or crumbled
1 tablespoon pork lard or olive oil
250g ready-cooked cornmeal porridge (polenta)
4 tablespoons chopped fresh parsley
1 tablespoon chopped fresh mint
Salt (optional)

1 Drain the beans and put them with the ham or bacon in a roomy, flameproof pot with the garlic, bay leaf, thyme sprig, peppercorns and enough cold water to cover; beans need plenty of room to swell. Bring to the boil, skim and simmer for about an hour, until they're perfectly soft. You may need to add a little boiling water during the cooking: the beans should be juicy but not quite soupy.

2 Meanwhile, fry the sliced *longaniza* or chorizo in a little lard or oil until browned at the edges, then remove and set aside. Chop the cornmeal porridge into dice and turn them in the pan drippings until they acquire a crisp little crust on all sides.

3 Stir the parsley and mint into the beans. Taste and add salt, if necessary. Top the beans with the *longaniza* or chorizo and serve the crisp cornmeal cubes on the side.

potage de lentejas

LENTIL SOUP WITH PORK AND GREENS

*L*entils, floury and nutty, are the fast food of the pulses since they don't need soaking. For a soup, choose the large, greeny-brown Spanish lentils which collapse in the pot drinking up the flavour of whatever else goes into the stew. French Puy lentils – smaller, darker, harder – are less suitable since they keep their shape after cooking and never really soften.

Serves 4

500g pork belly, diced
500g greeny-brown lentils
½ garlic head (about 6 fat cloves), unpeeled
2–3 links chorizo or 100g diced shoulder pork
and 1 tablespoon pimentón (Spanish paprika)
500g tomatoes (canned or fresh, roughly chopped)
½ teaspoon cumin seeds
Sea salt

TO FINISH
1 large potato, peeled and cubed
250g spring greens or spinach, shredded
2 tablespoons extra virgin olive oil
2–3 hard-boiled eggs (optional)

1 Trim the meat without discarding any fat – it adds flavour and the lentils will drink it all up. Pick over the lentils, checking for any tiny stones. Spear the garlic head on a knife and hold it in the gas flame (or light a candle), until the papery skin singes and blackens a little and the flesh is lightly caramelized.

2 Put everything except the finishing ingredients into a roomy saucepan with 2 litres water. Salt lightly and bring to the boil. Turn down the heat, cover loosely and leave to simmer gently for 40–50 minutes, until the lentils are perfectly soft and beginning to collapse into the broth. Stir occasionally to avoid sticking, and add a splash of boiling water if it looks like drying out.

3 When the lentils are tender, add the cubed potato. Return to the boil and turn down the heat. Cover again and cook for another 10 minutes, until the potato is nearly soft – test for doneness with a knife. Stir in the spring greens or spinach and bubble for another 5 minutes. Stir in the oil and bubble up again to amalgamate it with the broth – it disappears like magic, leaving a silky smoothness without a trace of oiliness. Taste and adjust the seasoning.

4 Ladle the soup into deep bowls and finish, if you like, with quartered hard-boiled eggs. Accompany with a young red wine, nothing grand – a little acidity aids the digestion.

chicken and barnyard

galantina de gallina

BONED STUFFED CHICKEN

A poached stuffed chicken, eaten cold and served in much the same way as the French pâté, is well worth the effort of boning out the bird. You'll find the commercially prepared version on the cold meats stall in Spanish markets, along with the serrano hams. In the days when every rural housewife kept hens for eggs, the chicken was not a roasting fowl but a gallina, an old hen past her laying days.

Serves 6–8

1 free-range chicken, about 1.5kg
500g minced pork (choose a fatty cut – shoulder or belly)
500g minced veal or young beef
About 150g fresh breadcrumbs
300ml white wine
2 eggs, lightly beaten
Salt and freshly milled black pepper
¼ teaspoon freshly grated nutmeg
1 onion, quartered
1 large carrot, cut into chunks
2–3 green (unblanched) celery sticks
1–2 bay leaves
½ teaspoon peppercorns

1 To bone out the chicken, lay the bird on its breast, back uppermost, and make a long slit with a sharp, slender-bladed knife right down the broad backbone.

2 Ease the flesh from the skeleton as if opening a book, first one side and then the other, using the knife to separate the skin and flesh from the carcass. Pull the flesh up the legs, severing the skin where it joins the drumsticks. Trim off the wings at the second joint – no need to bone them out.

3 Work your way up the carcass and over the breast, releasing the meat from the rib cage. Free the breastbone by slicing through the soft cartilage, keeping the skin intact.

4 Lay the boned-out chicken on the table with its flesh side uppermost. Remove most of the breast fillets and the thick part of the leg meat. Chop this roughly and mix with the minced meats and fresh breadcrumbs – enough to make a firm mixture.

5 Moisten with 2–3 tablespoons of the wine, work in the lightly beaten eggs and season with salt, freshly milled pepper and a little nutmeg.

6 Pat the mixture into a sausage shape and place on the boned-out chicken. Reform the casing over the stuffing, and sew up the openings with a sturdy needle and strong thread. Wrap in a clean cloth and tie or sew to make a neat chicken-shaped bolster.

7 Place the bolster in a roomy, flameproof pot just large enough to hold it comfortably. Add the remaining ingredients including the rest of the wine, and pour in enough water to submerge everything.

8 Add salt. Bring to the boil and turn down the heat. Cover and leave to simmer very gently for 90 minutes or so, until firm and cooked right through. Remove from the heat and leave to cool in its poaching water.

9 Once cooled, unwrap the gallatine and pack it into a loaf tin into which it will just fit. Weight down under a board and leave overnight in the fridge to firm and set.

SERVING SUGGESTION: cut into slices. As a starter or light summer lunch, serve with a potato salad dressed with a home-made mayonnaise.

In rural areas, care of the barnyard – the egg-layers, as well as rabbits for meat and the household pig for winter stores – was always the business of the woman of the household. In the outlying districts where smallholders grow most of the ingredients of the daily dinner, farmwives still keep a flock to provide the household with eggs, eating the meat only when the hen has outlived its usefulness. Elderly fowl, past their laying, go to make a rich, strong broth, whereas cockerels, duck and young geese, fattened on corn and leftovers, provide the festive dish for high days and holidays. Although in modern times, battery birds are as common as elsewhere in Europe, the Spanish chicken is a smallish breed. A barnyard fowl, accustomed to foraging for itself, is inevitably more muscular and tough than the hen-housed bird, and traditional Spanish cookery takes no risks, jointing the bird rather than cooking it whole.

pollo en ajopollo

CHICKEN WITH ALMONDS AND SAFFRON

*T*ender chicken cooked in a saffron sauce spiced with cinnamon and thickened with pounded almonds is a dish from the days of the Moors.

⋘⋙

Serves 4

1 chicken, jointed into about 12 pieces
Salt and freshly milled black pepper
4 tablespoons fresh pork lard or olive oil
2 garlic cloves, chopped
1 thick slice day-old bread
1 tablespoon chopped fresh parsley
2 tablespoons ground almonds
1 teaspoon ground cinnamon
½ teaspoon ground cloves
12 saffron threads soaked in 1 tablespoon boiling water
Juice and grated zest of 1 lemon
1 glass sherry or white wine (about 150ml)
1 large onion, finely sliced

TO FINISH (OPTIONAL)
1 tablespoon toasted flaked almonds

1 Trim the chicken joints, removing any whiskery feathers and flaps of skin, and season with salt and pepper.

2 Heat half the lard or oil in a frying pan and fry the garlic and bread until both are golden. Add the parsley and fry for a moment longer.

3 Transfer the contents of the pan to a food processor (or use a pestle and mortar) and process briefly. Add the ground almonds, cinnamon and cloves, the saffron and its soaking water, lemon juice and zest, and the sherry or wine. Continue to process to a smooth purée.

4 Meanwhile, reheat the pan and add the remaining lard or oil. Gently fry the onion and the chicken joints until the skin has browned a little and the onion is soft and golden. Stir in the nut purée and allow to bubble up. Cover, turn down the heat and simmer gently until the chicken joints are cooked right through and the sauce is concentrated to a couple of spoonfuls. Add a little boiling water only if needed. Taste and adjust the seasoning, if necessary.

5 Heap on a warm dish and sprinkle, if you like, with toasted flaked almonds.

pollo al ajillo

CHICKEN WITH GARLIC

This is the Andalusian housewife's way with a tender young chicken or hutch-reared rabbit. As with all simple things, the raw materials matter: the garlic should be firm and plump with no sign of sprouting; if using a chicken, pick a small free-range bird with a high ratio of bone to flesh – more chewable and easier to eat in your fingers. The olive oil must be mild and golden rather than green and leafy, since leafiness, so desirable on a salad, makes the oil taste bitter when subjected to high heat.

Serves 4

1 small free-range chicken, jointed into bite-sized pieces
1–2 tablespoons seasoned flour
About 8 tablespoons olive oil
8–12 garlic cloves, unpeeled
1 glass dry sherry or white wine (about 150ml)

1 Dust the chicken joints through the seasoned flour.

2 Heat the oil in a heavy frying pan. As soon as it's lightly hazed with blue, add the chicken joints, turn down the heat and fry gently for about 10 minutes, turning to brown all sides. Add the garlic cloves and fry them until the papery coverings brown a little, about another 5 minutes.

3 Add the sherry or wine and allow to bubble up until the steam no longer smells winey. Turn down the heat and simmer gently for another 15 minutes, until the chicken is cooked right through, the wine has completely evaporated, and the juices are reduced to a thick oily little dressing. To test the chicken for doneness, push a sharp knife through one of the thigh joints: when the juices run clear rather than pink, it's ready.

4 Allow to cool a little, serve with chunks of country bread and eat it with your fingers.

pollo con cigalas y calamares

CHICKEN WITH LANGOUSTINES AND SQUID

An elegant Catalan version of surf 'n' turf, this subtle little dish combines a tender young chicken with the most delicate of seafood. Prawns can replace the langoustines, but for a particularly luxurious version, use lobster instead (don't forget to include the coral from the head).

Serves 4–6

1 free-range chicken (about 1.5kg), jointed
1 tablespoon seasoned flour
300ml olive oil
250g langoustines (Dublin Bay prawns)
500g cuttlefish or squid, cleaned and sliced
1 medium onion, finely sliced
4 ripe tomatoes, skinned, deseeded and chopped
1 thyme sprig
1 bay leaf
1 slice day-old bread, crumbled
2–3 garlic cloves, chopped
1 tablespoon blanched almonds, roughly crushed
2 tablespoons brandy
Salt and freshly milled black pepper

1 Dust the chicken joints through the seasoned flour – drop everything into a plastic bag and shake it about for a moment.

2 Heat 1 tablespoon of the oil in a heavy sauté pan and fry the langoustines and cuttlefish or squid until the flesh turns opaque, then remove and set aside. Add 2 more tablespoons of oil to the pan and fry the chicken joints gently, turning to brown all sides, for 10 minutes, or until the meat firms, then remove and set aside.

3 Add another 2 tablespoons of oil to the pan and fry the onion gently for 15–20 minutes – take your time – until perfectly golden and soft. This is the basic *soffrito* of the Catalan kitchen.

4 Add the tomatoes and herbs, and allow to bubble up until the tomato collapses into a thick mush. Return the chicken joints to the pan, add enough water to almost submerge the pieces and bubble up again. Turn down the heat, cover loosely and leave to simmer for 15 minutes, or until the chicken is perfectly tender.

5 Meanwhile, in another pan, fry the crumbled bread in the remaining oil with the garlic and almonds until lightly browned. Add a spoonful of the cooking liquor to stop the cooking process, then crush the contents of the pan in a pestle and mortar or pulverize in the liquidizer. This is the *picada*, a basic preparation used by Catalan cooks to thicken and colour a sauce. (A rusk or a marie biscuit, crushed, can replace the breadcrumbs.)

6 Return the langoustines and cuttlefish or squid to the pan with the chicken and sauce, sprinkle with the brandy and bubble up until the steam no longer smells of alcohol.

7 Stir in the *picada* and bubble up to thicken – you may need a little more water. Taste and season with salt and freshly milled black pepper.

8 Remove the herbs and heap the chicken, fish and sauce onto a pretty dish.

SERVING SUGGESTION: serve with bread rubbed with oil and garlic, then toasted. A green salad – cos lettuce dressed with salt and lemon juice – will cut the richness.

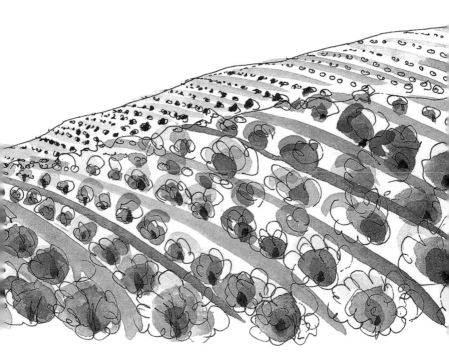

pavo chilindrón

TURKEY WITH RED PEPPERS

This is a classic dish from Saragossa in Aragón, where they grow particularly succulent red peppers. You can, if you prefer, make it with chicken or rabbit. If turkey is your choice, the robust flavour of the leg meat is preferable to the softer flesh of the breast. A pretty dish for a party.

Serves 6

1kg turkey meat, diced
2 garlic cloves, crushed
Salt and freshly milled black pepper
4 tablespoons olive oil
1 large mild onion, sliced into half-moons
6 red peppers, deseeded and sliced into strips
1 tablespoon diced ham
500g tomatoes, skinned and chopped
Small cinnamon stick
1 glass red wine (about 200ml)
Sugar (optional)

1 Fold the turkey meat with the garlic and season with salt and freshly milled black pepper.

2 Heat the oil in a roomy frying pan and add the onion and peppers. Fry until the vegetables soften and take a little colour, then turn down the heat and cook very gently for 20 minutes or so, until the water has evaporated and the vegetables are soft and thick.

3 Add the turkey meat and ham. Fry for 5–10 minutes, until the meat seizes and takes a little colour. Add the tomatoes, cinnamon and wine, and allow to bubble up until the steam no longer smells of alcohol.

4 Turn down the heat, cover tightly and simmer for 30–40 minutes – you may need to add a little more water if it looks like drying out – until the turkey meat is perfectly tender and the juices are well reduced. If it looks a little watery, remove the lid and bubble up fiercely for a minute or two, or until the sauce is thick and shiny. Taste and adjust the seasoning – you might need a little sugar if the tomatoes were not particularly ripe. Bubble up for a few minutes to marry the flavours.

5 Serve with white rice or plenty of bread. Good on the first day, better on the second.

oca con nabos y peras

GOOSE WITH TURNIPS AND PEARS

A *very popular dish, say Catalan cookbooks, which is open to many variations and is suitable for duck as well as goose. Catalans prefer a young gosling to the full grown goose, a bird which appears in the market at the end of September and whose season runs through October and November, growing larger by the day. By Christmas it's too large for jointing and is considered a little over the hill. The goose remains a resolutely seasonal bird, sticking to the natural calendar even when reared in the barnyard, where, incidentally, it earns its keep as a watchdog.*

Serves 4–6

1 young goose (about 2.5kg), jointed into about 12 pieces
Salt and freshly milled black pepper
2 large onions, finely sliced
500g tomatoes, skinned, deseeded and diced
1 tablespoon raisins, soaked to swell
Thyme sprig, marjoram sprig and bay leaf, tied in a bunch
1 short cinnamon stick
3–4 clove buds (the little balls at the end), crushed
in your fingers
150ml white wine
6 baby turnips, topped and tailed
12 small hard pears, peeled but uncored, with their stalks

THE FINISHING *PICADA*
2 tablespoons goose fat or pork lard
2 garlic cloves, chopped
2 tablespoons blanched almonds, crushed
1 slice day-old bread, crumbled
1 tablespoon pimentón (Spanish paprika) or the flesh from
2 dried peppers, soaked to soften
1 tablespoon white wine vinegar

1 Pick over the goose joints, removing and reserving the fat from the interior. Salt and pepper the joints, prick them all over with a fork and set them aside. Put the reserved fat in a flameproof earthenware casserole or heavy pan with a tablespoon of water, and cook gently until the fat melts and all the water has evaporate. Strain out the solids and return the drippings to the pan.

2 Fry the goose joints gently until the skin browns a little and the meat firms. Remove and set aside. Fry the onions very gently in the remaining drippings until they soften – don't let them take colour – allowing at least 15 minutes.

3 Add the tomatoes, raisins, herbs and spices and allow to bubble up until the tomato flesh collapses. Return the goose joints to the pan. Add the wine and bubble up to evaporate the alcohol. Season with salt and a little pepper, and add enough water to just submerge the joints. Bubble up again, then turn down the heat, cover loosely and cook until the goose is perfectly tender – 20–30 minutes should be enough as the the bird is young – and the sauce is well reduced.

4 Add the turnips and cook for 5 minutes. Slip in the pears, stalks pointing heavenwards, and cook for another 5–10 minutes, until the pears are tender but not mushy. Remove the goose and the pears to a warm serving dish. Remove and discard the little bunch of herbs and the cinnamon stick from the sauce.

5 Meanwhile, in another pan, make the finishing *picada*, a light thickening which adds flavour to the sauce. Heat the goose fat or lard in a small frying pan and fry the garlic, almonds and

crumbled bread until lightly browned. Sprinkle with the pimentón or the soaked dried pepper flesh and immediately add the vinegar. Bubble up for a moment to soften the acidity, then transfer the contents of the pan to a mortar and crush thoroughly with a pestle and mortar, or process in the liquidizer.

6 Stir the *picada* into the sauce and bubble up for a moment, stirring, until perfectly blended. Pour the sauce over the goose and around the pears – the pale flesh of the pears should still be visible. Serve with a lightly dressed frizzy endive salad – the bitterness of the leaves will balance the richness of the meat.

VARIATION: apples or plums can replace the pears, and you can omit the turnips altogether if you like.

pato con higos

DUCKLING WITH FIGS

*I*n *this recipe from the* caserios, *the sprawling farmhouses of the Basque country, a young duck is pot-roasted very gently with the local dry white wine,* tlaxcoli, *and finished with fresh figs. If these are not available, use dried figs soaked in hot water for an hour or two to swell.*

Serves 4

1 duckling (about 2kg)
Salt and freshly milled black pepper
1–2 bay leaves
1 small thyme sprig
1 tablespoon goose fat or pork lard
500g baby onions or small shallots
2 large carrots, diced
250ml dry white wine
500g fresh figs

1 Allow the bird to come up to room temperature first. Salt and pepper it inside and out, and tuck the bay leaves and thyme inside the cavity.

2 Preheat the oven to 160°C/325°F/Gas 3. Melt the goose fat or lard in a heavy, flameproof casserole large enough to accommodate the bird and the vegetables, and toss the onions or shallots over a gentle heat until browned.

3 Add the carrots and fry a little longer. Settle the duck breast-side down on top of the vegetables. Add the wine and pour in an equal volume of water (the liquid should nearly submerge the bird). Allow to bubble up briefly.

4 Cover tightly and transfer to the oven. Leave to cook for about 1½ hours, until perfectly tender: when the duck's leg joint can be wiggled in its socket and the juices run clear when pierced with a skewer, it's ready. Remove the bird and its vegetables to a warm serving dish. Joint the duck into quarters.

5 Place the figs gently in the juices in the pan, bubble up, turn down the heat, cover tightly and cook for 5 minutes, until the figs are heated right through. Arrange the figs around the duck. Reduce the juices in the pan to a concentrated slick of sauce, taste and season with salt and pepper, and pour over the duck.

pato con guisantes

DUCKLING WITH PEAS

A recipe from the Atlantic regions of northern Spain, dairy country, where the whey from the butter and cheese-making is used to fatten the pig, and the climate, being rainy and cool even in summer, suits both ducks and peas. The hams from these regions are softer and milder in flavour than the chewy serrano hams found elsewhere.

Serves 4

1 smallish duck (about 1.5kg), jointed
1 tablespoon lard or butter
100g small shallots or baby onions, left whole
2 tablespoons diced serrano ham
300ml dry cider
Salt and freshly milled black pepper
450g podded peas

1 Prick the duck joints all over with a fork to allow the fat to run. Melt the lard or butter in a heavy, flameproof casserole that will comfortably accommodate the duck. Brown the bird all over in the hot butter: this will take 10–15 minutes.

2 Remove the duck joints and set aside (if the pan is sufficiently roomy, just push them to one side). Add the shallots or onions to the oily residue in the pan and fry until they begin to brown.

3 Return the duck joints to the pan, add the ham and cider and allow to bubble up for a minute or two. Season with salt and pepper. Turn down the heat to a gentle simmer. Cover and cook for 20 minutes. Add the peas. Cook for another 10 minutes or so, until the peas have lost their brilliant green and the duck joints are perfectly tender. To test for doneness, insert a skewer into one of the thigh joints: when the juices run clear, it's ready.

meat

chuletas de ternera a la parilla con salsa de avellanas

GRILLED STEAKS ON THE BONE WITH HAZELNUT SALSA

*I*n the Basque Country, young beef, ternera – *in the form of thick steaks on the bone – is the great luxury, a taste that can only be satisfied by a trip to one of the* asadores *which specialize in grilled meats and nothing else; well, maybe a spoonful of sauce and a hunk of bread. Traditionally, the beef came from the gentle black cattle used to pull the plough across the steep hillsides, although most of the meat now comes from the* rubio gallego, *Galicia's red cattle, or from the black-coated herds of the bull ranches of Andalusia. T-bone steaks cut from young beef (older than veal) come closest to the real thing.*

Serves 4

4 T-bone steaks
1–2 tablespoons olive oil
1 garlic clove, finely minced
Salt and freshly milled black pepper

THE SALSA
100g toasted hazelnuts (skinned or not, as you please)
1 shallot or small onion, roughly chopped
2 tablespoons cider vinegar
4 tablespoons finely chopped fresh parsley
4 tablespoons olive oil

1 Wipe over the steaks and rub the surfaces with oil. Sprinkle with garlic and season with salt and pepper. Leave at room temperature for an hour or two to take the flavours.

2 Meanwhile, light the barbecue or heat the grill while you make the salsa.

3 For the salsa, put all the ingredients except the oil into a liquidizer with a tablespoon of water, and reduce to a smooth purée. Add the oil gradually as if making a mayonnaise, until the

sauce thickens. If it's a hot day, add a dry crust of bread to maintain the emulsion.

4 Grill the meat over a fierce heat, turning it once, until done to your liking. To test for doneness, prod the meat with your finger – if it feels soft, the meat will be rare, if the surface still has a little elasticity, it will be medium done, if firm, it's well done. To check, place your forefinger on the tip of your thumb and feel the firmness of the thumb ball; replace the forefinger with the second finger and feel again, and so on until you reach the little finger. The forefinger produces the softest thumb ball, corresponding to meat cooked rare, and the little finger produces the hardest, corresponding to well-done.

5 Serve each steak with a thick slab of bread and hand round the salsa separately. Cider is the appropriate accompaniment: this is apple country.

Hunger is the best sauce.

Spanish saying

filete a la milanesa

BREADED ESCALOPES

Thrifty Spanish cooks would be lost without this easy way to make a little go a long way. There was a time when fresh meat, a luxury until modern and more prosperous times, was eaten only on Sundays, and even then only by city folk. Spain's butchers take an economical view of their duties, automatically boning out their carcasses and dividing the meat according to the muscle formation. These large rounds of meat are then sliced thinly and sold as filete, escalopes, a term which can apply equally to pork, veal or beef, although the latter is eaten young and unhung, while still tender.

Serves 4

500g veal, beef or pork escalopes
2 tablespoons seasoned flour
2 eggs
2 tablespoons milk
4 heaped tablespoons home-made fresh breadcrumbs
Olive oil, for deep-frying

TO SERVE
1 quartered lemon

1 Place each escalope between two sheets of clingfilm and flatten with a rolling pin. The meat should be extremely thin.

2 Spread the seasoned flour on one plate, beat the eggs and milk together on another and spread the breadcrumbs on a third. Dust the escalopes through the flour (shake off the excess), then flip them through the egg and milk to coat both sides. Press well into the breadcrumbs, making sure both surfaces are well-jacketed.

3 Heat a finger's depth of oil in a frying pan – you'll need just enough depth to submerge the meat. The oil should be hot but not yet smoking – test with a bread cube, which should form bubbles around the edges and become golden within a moment. Slip in the escalopes one or two at a time, so that the temperature doesn't drop. Turn to fry the other side. Transfer to kitchen paper to drain. Serve with the lemon quarters.

SERVING SUGGESTION: mashed potato, beaten with oil rather than butter and flavoured with ground allspice, is the perfect accompaniment.

picadillo valenciana

MINCEMEAT WITH SAFFRON AND RAISINS

Moorish spicing and a touch of sweetness enlivens Monday's mince: I loved this dish when I was a teenager in Madrid. My mother's cook came from Valencia and included saffron, cinnamon and raisins whenever she could.

Serves 4

750g minced meat (best done by hand with a knife, but no matter)
1 tablespoon finely diced serrano ham
2 tablespoons olive oil
1 large onion, diced
1 large carrot, diced
1 garlic clove, peeled
6–8 saffron threads
Salt and freshly milled black pepper
2 large ripe tomatoes, skinned, deseeded and diced
or 2 tablespoons tomato purée
1 tablespoon raisins
500g potatoes, peeled and cut into bite-sized cubes
½ teaspoon ground cinnamon
1 bay leaf

TO FINISH
1 tablespoon toasted pine nuts
2 hard-boiled eggs, quartered

1 Mix the meat with the ham. Heat the oil in a flameproof casserole or heavy saucepan. When it is good and hot, stir in the meat, diced onion and carrot and let everything cook gently until it loses its water, begins to fry and takes a little colour.

2 Meanwhile, crush the garlic and saffron with a little salt, dilute with a splash of water and stir this paste into the meat as soon as it begins to fry.

3 Add the tomatoes and bubble up until the flesh softens and collapses or stir in the tomato purée. Add the raisins, potatoes, cinnamon and bay leaf, and turn to blend with the meat. Add enough water to just cover everything.

4 Bubble up again and turn down the heat. Cover loosely and leave to simmer gently for 25–30 minutes, or until the meat is tender and the potatoes are soft. Taste and adjust the seasoning, turn up the heat and let it bubble up to evaporate the extra moisture – it should be juicy but not soupy.

5 Finish with a sprinkle of toasted pine nuts and quartered hard-boiled eggs. Perfect spoon food for toothless grannies and hungry children.

guiso de ternera mechada

BRAISED VEAL WITH SERRANO HAM

Veal – in Spain, this is usually young beef rather than milk-fed calf – is naturally dry and mild flavoured. It benefits from larding – threading the meat with strips of fatty pork or some other meat – which adds richness and flavour.

Serves 6–8

**2kg boned-out veal or young beef, rolled and tied as
for a pot-roast
50g thick-cut serrano ham with plenty of golden fat
500g mature carrots
4 tablespoons olive oil
500g shallots or baby onions
4 garlic cloves, crushed with a little salt
125g mushrooms (wild is best), sliced
A few thyme sprigs, oregano sprigs, bay leaf
½ teaspoon crushed black pepper
¼ teaspoon crushed allspice
1 bottle red wine
Salt
A little sugar**

1 Insert a sharp knife right through the heart of the joint to make a deep incision from end to end – starting at the blunt end, the knife point should appear at the tip. Cut the ham into matchsticks and cut one of the carrots into narrow batons. Push the ham and carrot batons into the incisions of the joint – be patient, use a skewer or a larding needle to help you on your way.

2 Preheat the oven to 150°C/300°F/Gas 2. Heat the oil in a roomy flameproof casserole and brown the meat on all sides. Pack in the shallots or onions, garlic and remaining carrots, cut into chunks to the same size as the onions. Add the mushrooms.

3 Tuck in the herbs (in a little bunch, if that's convenient) and the spices. Add the wine and season with salt and a little sugar to balance the acidity of the wine.

4 Bring to the boil, remove from the heat and cover tightly – use foil as well as a lid. Transfer the casserole to the oven. Leave to cook gently in its own juices for 2–3 hours – overnight is not too long, although, if this is your choice, you should drop the temperature to 140°C/275°F/Gas 1.

5 When perfectly tender, remove and leave to rest before slicing. Serve at room temperature, with its sauce.

cordero estofado en salsa de almendras

POT-ROAST LAMB WITH ALMONDS

A recipe from the shepherding regions of Spain – anywhere north of Andalusia. Lamb on the bone flavoured with garlic and finished with a thick paste of toasted almonds and pimentón. In the lands of the south, where the goat is the usual milk animal, it's made with kid – meat which is somewhat hard to come by unless you're round the Mediterranean.

Serves 4

**1.5kg thick lamb steaks (shoulder or leg), chopped right across
the bone
Salt and freshly milled black pepper
200g whole unblanched almonds
4 tablespoons olive oil
1 whole head garlic (about a dozen cloves), broken but
not peeled
1–2 bay leaves
1 thyme sprig
200ml white wine or dry sherry
1 tablespoon pimentón (Spanish paprika), smoked, for preference,
1 tablespoon toasted flaked almonds (optional)**

1 Wipe over the lamb and season with salt and pepper.

2 Toast the almonds gently in a heavy earthenware or enamel flameproof casserole with a teaspoon of oil; as soon as the skins loosen and the nuts begin to brown, remove and set aside.

3 Reheat the casserole with the remaining oil and fry the meat, turning to brown all sides. Add the garlic cloves and fry for another few minutes. Add the herbs, wine or sherry and the same value of water, and allow to bubble up.

4 Turn down the heat and leave to simmer gently, loosely covered, for 1 hour, until the meat is tender enough to eat with a spoon. Or transfer to the oven and cook at 160°C/325°F/ Gas 3 for the same amount of time. Check occasionally and add another glassful of water if necessary. The cooking broth should be well reduced by the end, but the meat should never be allowed to dry out.

5 Remove a spoonful of the broth, put it with the reserved almonds and pimentón (Spanish paprika) into a liquidizer (or use a pestle and mortar), and pound to a paste. Stir the paste into the cooking juices and bubble up again to thicken.

6 Heap everything onto a warm serving dish and finish, if you like, with toasted flaked almonds.

caldereta de piernas de cordero

BRAISED LAMB SHANKS

The shank – the end piece of the shoulder – cooks to a gluey softness when subject to gentle braising. Although the cooking time is long, the preparation is short – slow food at its most succulent. You can leave it, tightly covered, in a low oven overnight and it will come to no harm.

Serves 4

4 lamb shanks
Salt
2 tablespoons olive oil
1 tablespoon diced serrano ham or lean bacon
250g small shallots or baby onions
1 large carrot, chunked
500g ripe tomatoes, skinned, deseeded and diced
2–3 garlic cloves, crushed with a little salt
1–2 rosemary sprigs
1–2 thyme sprigs
½ teaspoon peppercorns, crushed
1 generous glass dry sherry or white wine (about 200ml)

1 Wipe over the meat and season with salt. Preheat the oven to 150°C/300°F/Gas 2.

2 Heat the oil in a roomy flameproof earthenware or enamel casserole that will just accommodate the lamb shanks in a single layer. Brown the meat lightly, turning to sear on all sides. Settle the shanks bone-end upwards.

3 Add the remaining ingredients, packing them around the sides of the casserole. Bring all to the boil, cover tightly (seal with a layer of foil, shiny side downwards, if you're uncertain about the fit) and transfer to the oven.

4 Leave to cook gently for at least 3 hours – longer if that's more convenient – without unsealing, unless your nose and ears tell you the meat is beginning to fry, when you'll need to add a splash of water. The meat should be tender enough to eat with a spoon and the sauce reduced to a thick jammy slick – very delicious indeed.

empanada gallega

SPICED PORK AND ONION PIE

A juicy meat pie spiced with pimentón and baked between two layers of pastry makes excellent picnic food. Whereas other regions have their own versions, this particular filling is typically Galician. Although the pastry can be one of your own choosing, a yeast pastry is more common in the region.

Serves 4–6

THE PASTRY

300g strong bread flour, plus extra for dusting
¹⁄₂ teaspoon salt
1 teaspoon easy-blend dried yeast
4 tablespoons oil, plus extra for oiling
1 tablespoon beaten egg, for glazing

THE FILLING

300g diced lean pork
1 tablespoon pimentón (Spanish paprika)
¹⁄₂ tablespoon dried oregano
1 garlic clove, crushed
2 tablespoons olive oil
1 medium onion, diced
2 red peppers, deseeded and diced
¹⁄₂ glass white wine (about 75ml)
¹⁄₂ teaspoon saffron threads, soaked in a little water
500g tomatoes, skinned, deseeded and diced
1 tablespoon diced serrano ham or lean bacon
1 teaspoon dried thyme
2–3 anchovy fillets, chopped
¹⁄₂ teaspoon chilli flakes
Salt (if necessary)

1 Make the pastry first. Sieve the flour with salt into a warm bowl and mix in the dried yeast. Make a well in the middle and pour in 150ml warm water. Sprinkle the surface with a handful of flour and leave for 10 minutes in a warm place to allow the yeast to begin working. Add the oil (it should be as warm as your hand), and work the dry and wet ingredients together with the hook of your hand until you have soft elastic dough. Drop the ball back into the bowl, cover the bowl with clingfilm and set in a warm place for an hour or two until doubled in size.

2 Meanwhile, make the filling. Trim the meat and turn it with the pimentón or paprika, oregano and garlic. Heat half the oil in a frying pan and gently fry the meat until it stiffens and browns a little. Remove and reserve.

3 Reheat the pan with the remaining oil and fry the onion and peppers until they soften, about at least 10 minutes. Add the wine, saffron, tomatoes, diced ham, thyme and anchovies. Bubble up for a moment.

4 Return the meat to the pan and bubble up again. Cover loosely and simmer until the liquid has evaporated and the meat is tender, about 20 minutes. Taste and add chilli and salt if necessary (the anchovies provide salt). Leave aside to cool while you finish the pastry.

5 Preheat the oven to 180°C/350°F/Gas 4. Knock back the dough to distribute the air bubbles by punching it with your fist. Knead until elastic and springy – you'll feel the dough continue to rise as you work. Cut the dough in two – one piece should be a little larger than the other.

6 Brush a baking tray (about 34 x 22cm) with oil and dust with a little flour (non-stick needs no such attention). Work each piece of dough into a smooth ball.

7 On a floured surface, pat out or roll each ball to form two rectangles, one roughly the same size as the baking tray, one a little smaller. Lay the larger piece in the baking tray, bringing it comfortably up the sides.

8 Spread the filling over the pastry in an even layer. Dampen the edges of the pastry, and top with the remaining dough. Work the two edges together in a rope pattern with a damp finger. Prick the top in a few places with a fork and paint with the egg to give the pie a pretty glaze.

9 Bake for 40–50 minutes, or until the pastry is well risen and browned. Serve at room temperature.

estofado de rabo de buey

SPICED OXTAIL HOTPOT

Oxtail dishes are still found wherever there was once a leather-working industry, since the skins for the trade came in with the tail still attached – a free perk for the leather workers. This delicious version, perfumed with the spices beloved by the Moors, is how they like it in city of Cordova, famed for hand-tooled leather since the days when Andalusia was ruled from Baghdad. The use of Eastern spices in savoury stews is common to all those regions where the Moorish influence was strong. After the Reconquest, when Granada, last of the Caliphates, fell to the combined crowns of Ferdinand of Aragon and Isabel of Castile, the people's appetite for the flavours of the sun – cinnamon, cloves, nutmeg – remained.

Serves 4–6

1–2 oxtails (depending on size), cut into sections
2 tablespoons olive oil
1 tablespoon diced serrano ham or lean bacon
1 large onion, diced
2 garlic cloves, crushed with a little salt
1 green celery stick, chopped
1 large carrot, scrubbed and diced
500g ripe tomatoes, skinned, deseeded and diced
1 tablespoon hot pimentón (Spanish chilli powder)
1 small cinnamon stick
½ teaspoon crushed allspice
3–4 cloves
1 bay leaf
1 bottle rough red wine
Salt and freshly milled black pepper

1 Rinse the oxtail and trim off excess fat. Heat the oil in a flame-proof casserole that will comfortably accommodate all the pieces.

2 Preheat the oven to 150°C/300°F/Gas 2. Turn the oxtail pieces in the hot oil until the edges brown a little. Remove from the casserole. Add the diced ham or bacon, onion, garlic, celery and carrot to the casserole and fry gently until the vegetables soften. Add the tomatoes, the spices and bay leaf. Allow to bubble up to

soften the tomatoes. Add the red wine and bubble up again until the steam no longer smells winey.

3 Return the oxtail to the pot and add enough water to barely cover all the pieces. Season with salt and freshly milled black pepper. Bring back to the boil, turn down the heat, cover tightly and transfer to the oven (or leave to cook on a very low heat) for 3–4 hours, or until the meat is falling off the bones. Check from time to time and add more water if necessary.

4 To finish, transfer the oxtail to a warm serving dish and bubble up the juices in the pot to concentrate the flavour. Check the seasoning. You can, if you like, stir in a ladleful of cooked chickpeas to make the oxtail go further. Good today, even better tomorrow.

⌒◯⌒

The tint in which Goya dipped his brush was negro de hueso, *bone-black, a pigment every Spanish painter extracted from serrano-ham bones baked to a rich burnt umber in the* olla-pot *– a symbol of plenty in the good times, and of deprivation when times were hard…The fat [of serrano-ham] looks like melted topazes.*

Richard Ford, *Gatherings from Spain*

higado encebollada

LIVER AND ONIONS

A great deal of onion makes a sauce for the tender meat, which is cooked rare. A classic combination from the Basque Country, very simple and very good.

Serves 4

500g finely sliced veal liver
1–2 tablespoons milk
4 tablespoons pork lard or butter
500g onions, finely sliced
Salt and freshly milled black pepper
1 heaped tablespoon seasoned flour
½ teaspoon fennel seeds

1 Cut the liver into fine strips and set it to soak in a little milk for half an hour.

2 Heat 3 tablespoons of the lard or butter in a heavy frying pan. Add the onions, salt lightly and let them cook very slowly for 25–30 minutes, turning them regularly, until soft and lightly caramelized. Remove to a sieve to catch the drippings.

3 Drain the liver strips and flip them quickly through the seasoned flour. Reheat the pan with the remaining lard or butter and the drippings from the sieve. Drop in the liver and sear the strips briefly but fiercely, shaking the pan so that the heat reaches all sides, allowing no more than a couple of minutes.

4 Return the onions to the pan and sprinkle with the fennel seeds. Turn to blend the onion and the meat and cook gently for another 5 minutes to blend the flavours. That's all.

Pork is the most popular and widely available meat in Spanish markets. The omniverous pig – in his lean, red-bristled Iberian incarnation, a descendant of the last foraging herds of Europe – has long been an honoured member of the Spanish rural household. As well as being allowed to range wild through the woods to scavenge for roots and acorns, he was a useful recycler of kitchen leftovers, vegetable peelings and anything edible that would otherwise go to waste – until, that is, Brussels decided this uncontrollable diet was not to be tolerated. Even so, the annual pig-killing still provides isolated farming communities with their winter supplies of wind-dried ham and spicy chorizo sausages. In what was once Muslim Spain, which included Andalusia, pork was a dietary taboo until the Christian Reconquest at the end of the fifteenth century.

Young beef from an animal halfway between veal and mature bullock is the preferred meat for grilling and frying. Spanish butchers are adept at boning out and slicing up virtually the whole animal – from rump to skirt to shoulder – into thin escalopes somewhat confusingly described as fillet (*filete*). The alternative is a piece of shin, or a choice of innards including the testicles. Spanish cooks believe that every bit of the animal should be both admired and eaten – and quite right too. Bull meat, sold cheap in the marketplace after the bullfight, was once the only meat the urban poor might taste.

Lamb is eaten wherever sheep are kept for milk, meat and wool – the Basque Country and Catalonia as well as the high central plateau, where the searing heat of summer gives way to bone-chilling winters. In the south, Andalusia, where lamb was the preferred meat of the Moors, sheep meat almost disappeared from the menu after the Reconquest. Four centuries after the caliphs left Granada, in the 1970s, the butcher in Tarifa, my local market town in Spain's southernmost tip, couldn't or wouldn't sell lamb to his customers. Why? '*Es carne de Moro*' ('It's Moorish meat'). At the same time, in the streets of Tarifa married ladies went about half-veiled in the Muslim style, with headscarves covering the hair and then wrapped across the lower part of the face.

Kid, the meat of young male goats is the great treat among the rural communities of the Spanish heartland. In Castile and Aragón, Andalusia and the Levant, the hardy goat, suited to the territory and able to survive on very little fodder and even less water, is the main milk animal. Kid, roasted in the bread oven or as a savoury stew, marks the high spot of the country wedding feast, a roofing-out party or any occasion where the food must be special.

Offal and mince are the traditional source of cheap protein among the urban poor and city dwellers who lacked access to the meat-animals – game, poultry, pigs – that were available to country dwellers, landlord permitting.

game

pichones con ajos

BRAISED PIGEONS WITH GARLIC

The garlicky sweet–sour sauce is a perfect match for the gamey flavour of the wild birds. Pigeons, one of the neglected pleasures of the game larder, were poor-man's meat, netted or shot when they came home to roost after a day's gleaning in the landlord's fields. Baby poussin or farmed quail are the alternatives.

Serves 4–8

8 pigeons, cleaned and wiped
Salt and freshly milled black pepper
6 tablespoons olive oil
2 onions, finely sliced
24 fat garlic cloves, whole and unpeeled
250ml red wine
1 tablespoon red wine vinegar
1 tablespoon raisins
2 bay leaves
1 short cinnamon stick
2–3 cloves

1 Pick over the pigeons for any stray feathers or whiskers, and pat them dry. Salt them inside and out.

2 Heat the oil in a heavy, flameproof casserole with a tight-fitting lid. Put in the pigeons and turn them in the hot oil until the skin takes a little colour, then remove and reserve.

3 Add the onions and garlic, and fry gently for about 15 minutes, until softened and golden – don't let the onions brown. Return the pigeons to the casserole.

4 Pour in the wine and bubble vigorously to evaporate the alcohol. Add the remaining ingredients and a glassful of water (about 150ml), and reheat until boiling.

5 Turn down the heat, cover tightly and either transfer to a gentle oven – 160°C/325°F/Gas 3 – or leave to simmer for at least an hour, or until the birds are tender enough to eat with a spoon. Check at intervals, baste the birds, and add a little more boiling water if necessary.

6 Transfer the birds to a warm serving dish. Bubble up the cooking juices to concentrate the flavours. Spoon the sauce over the birds.

7 Best eaten with the fingers, with bread for mopping. The garlic cloves, mild and sweet after the long cooking, can be popped out of their papery jackets straight into your mouth.

codornices con col

PARTRIDGES WITH CABBAGE

This classic combination is a countryman's dish for the autumn, when the first cabbages of the year form their firm green drum-heads, partridges grow fat in the vineyards and the woods are full of wild fungi – boletuses, chanterelles and orange tears. The recipe also works well with guinea fowl – two birds will serve the same amount of diners.

Serves 4

4 partridges
1 tablespoon seasoned flour
6 tablespoons olive oil
1 large onion, finely chopped
1 large carrot, diced
100g wild or cultivated mushrooms, wiped and sliced
1 tablespoon diced serrano ham
1 generous glass red wine (about 300ml)
1 thyme sprig
1 bay leaf
Salt and freshly milled black pepper
1 medium-sized green cabbage, shredded

1 Pick over the birds and remove any stray whiskers. Dust with a little seasoned flour to protect the delicate skin.

2 Heat the oil in a heavy, flameproof casserole and brown the birds gently on all sides. Remove and reserve. Add the onion and carrot to the hot oil and fry gently until they soften and become golden – don't let them brown. Add the mushrooms and ham, and fry until the fungi lose their water and begin to sizzle. Add the wine, thyme and bay leaf, and allow to bubble up for a few minutes to evaporate the alcohol.

3 Return the birds to the casserole, add a glass of water (about 150ml), bubble up again, and then turn down the heat. Cover tightly and leave to stew gently for 40–60 minutes, depending on the age and size of the birds, until perfectly tender – test by wiggling a drumstick in its socket. Remove the birds and keep warm.

4 Reheat the pan juices, taste and season with salt and freshly milled black pepper, and add the shredded cabbage. Bubble up, cover tightly and steam fiercely for 3–4 minutes, or until the cabbage is just tender but still bright green. Remove the cabbage with a draining spoon and heap it onto a warm serving dish. Top with the partridges and sauce with the pan juices – they may need a quick bubble to concentrate the flavour.

conejo con ciruelas pasas

RABBIT WITH PRUNES

A recipe from the Basque Country, where rabbits fatten in the orchards and the year's crop of plums are dried for winter stores. If preparing the rabbit yourself, don't forget to lift off the bluish membrane which covers the back and legs – use a sharp knife – or the meat will never be tender. The recipe works almost as well with duck or chicken. If you happen to have a bottle of pacharán, Basque plum brandy, add a splash at the end of the cooking and set it alight to burn off the alcohol. It does wonders for the flavour.

Serves 4–6

1 large hutch rabbit (2 if wild and small), jointed
2 tablespoons seasoned flour
2 tablespoons pork lard or butter
250g small onions or shallots
3–4 garlic cloves, roughly chopped
300ml red wine
1 thyme sprig
1–2 bay leaves
2–3 cloves
1 short cinnamon stick
250g prunes, soaked to swell
Salt and freshly milled black pepper

1 Dust the rabbit joints through seasoned flour.

2 Heat the lard or butter in a roomy casserole and fry the onions or shallots and garlic and fry gently until they take a little colour. Push to one side and turn the rabbit joints in the hot fat and let them brown a little.

3 Add the wine, herbs and spices and a glass or two of water – just enough to cover everything. Allow to bubble up, turn down the heat, and cover loosely. Leave to simmer gently for an hour, until the meat is perfectly tender. Check every now and then in case you need to add a little more water.

4 After half an hour, add the prunes. Remove the lid at the end and bubble up to reduce the juices to a shiny little sauce. Taste and adjust the seasoning.

SERVING SUGGESTION: serve in the cooking dish, or pile everything on a warm serving platter. Eat with a spoon and use your fingers – no one can eat a bony little rabbit with a knife and fork.

pato a la sevillana

WILD DUCK WITH OLIVES AND ORANGES

The wetlands of the Guadalquivir and those of Valencia attract all manner of overwintering duck, an attraction for the hunters. You may, if you prefer, make this with a domestic duck, quartered. Sevillan or marmalade oranges, thin-skinned and sharp, are available only in January and February. At other times of the year, use lemons or limes.

Serves 4

2 mallard, quartered, or 4 smaller wild duck, halved
2 tablespoons olive oil
2 garlic cloves, finely chopped
2 tablespoons diced serrano ham
1 teaspoon ground cinnamon
½ teaspoon ground cloves
1 tablespoon green olives, pitted or not as you please
2 bitter oranges or 2 small, thin-skinned lemons, diced
1 glass dry sherry or white wine (about 150ml)
Salt and freshly milled black pepper

1 Wipe the duck joints and season with pepper. Trickle with 1 tablespoon oil and sprinkle with garlic. Leave for 30 minutes to take the flavours.

2 Heat the remaining oil in a heavy, flameproof casserole and gently fry the duck joints until the skin takes a little colour.

3 Add the diced ham, spices, olives and the chopped citrus fruit, and turn all over the heat for a minute or two.

4 Pour in the sherry or white wine and just enough water to cover, and allow to bubble up. Cover loosely, turn down the heat and leave to simmer gently for 30–40 minutes, or until the birds are perfectly tender and the sauce reduced to a thick, rich citrus sludge. Taste and add salt if necessary (the ham and olives are already salty).

SERVING SUGGESTION: good with crisp twice-fried chips cooked in olive oil and a salad of curly endive tossed, as they like it in Seville, with a little sherry vinegar, olive oil, coarse salt and a few sprigs of tarragon.

venado estofado con chocolate

VENISON STEWED WITH CHOCOLATE

*F*urry game is always improved by a night in a marinade: the meat is invariably lean and dry, and the flavours must be well developed to be convincing. The chocolate is used at the end to thicken and darken the sauce, much as the blood would do if you are making a civet.

Serves 4

1kg shoulder venison, diced

THE MARINADE
1 bottle red wine
2 tablespoons olive oil
1 tablespoon sherry or red wine vinegar
2 garlic cloves, crushed
1–2 bay leaves
1 teaspoon crushed allspice berries
$\frac{1}{2}$ teaspoon crushed peppercorns
$\frac{1}{2}$ teaspoon salt

2 tablespoons oil
1 thick slice serrano ham fat or fatty bacon, cubed
500g baby onions or shallots
1 large carrot, diced
50g bitter black chocolate, grated
Salt and freshly milled black pepper
1 tablespoon blanched, flaked almonds

1 Put the diced venison in a bowl and cover with the marinade, turning to blend. Leave overnight in a cool place – 2 days is even better.

2 Next day, remove the venison from the marinade, drain and shake dry, reserving the marinade.

3 Heat a tablespoon of oil in a deep saucepan and put in the cubed ham fat or bacon, half the onions or shallots, and the diced carrot. Let everything fry for a few minutes, and then push it all to one side and put in the meat (first you can dust the pieces with flour if you like a thicker sauce). Let the meat seize and brown a little in the hot oil.

4 Add the marinade with all its bits, allow everything to bubble up and turn down the heat. Leave to simmer gently, loosely covered, for an hour or so, until the venison is quite tender. You

may need to add a little water – not too much since you want a thick, rich sauce. Ten minutes before end of the cooking, stir in the grated chocolate and bubble up to blend and thicken. Taste and adjust the seasoning.

5 Meanwhile, cook the remaining onions or shallots gently in a closed pan with the remaining oil until they are golden and tender, then remove and reserve. Fry the almonds gently in the pan drippings until golden.

6 Heap the meat on a warm serving dish, spoon over the sauce and finish with the onions and almonds.

NOTE: Chocolate, in its original form, was a fortifying infusion considered to have magical properties prepared from the fermented, roasted, pounded seeds of the cacao tree, a native of the Central Americas. Spain had it first, stolen from the court of Monteczuma, last emperor of the Aztecs, whose ritual food it was. In the form in which it was taken – unsweetened, thickened with maize-flour, spiced with chilli – it served as a symbol of the sacrifice of human blood. Naturally enough for a foodstuff with such a pedigree, it's used instead of fresh blood in a civet, a convenient replacement for the traditional thickening-agent. In Spain as well as Italy and France (as well as the classier chocolate outlets elsewhere), unsweetened chocolate for use in savoury dishes is available in both powder and tablet-form.

codornices a la parilla con salsa verde

GRILLED QUAIL WITH PARSLEY AND GARLIC SAUCE

When I first set up home in a remote Spanish valley with my young family in the early 1960's, our neighbours cheerfully slaughtered by fair means or foul (mostly the latter) all things which had feathers and flew. Small birds were left to small boys, and my son, finding new friends in the local schoolroom, swiftly learned their tricks. These gatherings – food for free – were swiftly plucked and skewered (no point in gutting) and roasted over a brushfire of juniper, rosemary and thyme. The small victims – no more than a mouthful each – were delicious, no question, but good sense and the appearance on TV of a popular wild-life programme soon put a stop to the practice, leaving bird-populations already depleted by loss of habitat to recover as best they might. The farmed quail which replaced the song-birds – delicate meat, pale and tender and inclined to blandness – takes well to a robust parsley-and-garlic sauce from the Basque Country.

Serves 4

THE BIRDS
8 spatchcocked quails

THE MARINADE
2 tablespoons olive oil
Juice of 1 lemon
2 garlic cloves, finely slivered
1 tablespoon dried oregano
Salt and freshly milled black pepper

THE SAUCE
2 slices country bread, crusts removed, soaked
and squeezed dry
2 garlic cloves, roughly crushed with a little salt
300ml chopped fresh flat-leaf parsley, about 150g
2 tablespoons white wine or sherry vinegar
150ml olive oil

1 Thread the quails on skewers to keep them spread out flat. Sprinkle both sides with the marinade ingredients and set aside to take the flavours for an hour or two at room temperature or overnight in the fridge.

2 Preheat the grill or heat the oven to maximum. Grill or roast the birds for 10 minutes on one side. Turn, baste and allow another 5–8 minutes on the other, until the flesh is firm and the skin beautifully browned. Test by pushing a larding needle or fine skewer into the breast and thigh of one of the birds – the juices should run clear.

3 Meanwhile, make the sauce. Put all the ingredients except the oil in the liquidizer and process to a thick purée, then add the oil slowly in a thin stream, as if making a mayonnaise, until you have a creamy sauce. If it splits, a splash of boiling water will bring it back.

SERVING SUGGESTION: serve the birds on thick slabs of toasted country bread to catch the drippings, with the sauce handed round separately.

NOTE: to spatchcock quail (or any other bird), split the carcass in half right down the back, open it out and press firmly on the breastbone to flatten – it'll look like a squashed frog but cook in double-quick time.

Wild meat – both furred and feathered – is much prized for flavour and leanness in the Spanish kitchen. Large game – wild boar and deer – were traditionally the landlord's property, whereas the smaller game animals – rabbits, pigeons and those birds not considered suitable for the landlord's gun – were left for the poor. The Iberian peninsula is still rich in plains game, although much of the land is no longer wooded and the forests have retreated to mountain areas too rocky to support agriculture. The Spanish huntsman does not like to eat his game 'high' – not least because the warmth of summer quickly leads to spoiling – preferring to eat it straight from the field, slow-cooked for succulence. The game stews prepared in the Spanish kitchen are designed to add flavour and richness to meat of uncertain age and tenderness. Wild duck, pigeon and partridge – both red legged and grey legged – are the most plentiful of Spain's feathered game; bustard and quail have almost vanished. Among sophisticates and rural communities who continue to cook as their grandmothers did, even smaller game is much appreciated: in Andalusia, snails no larger than a thumbnail are gathered in the bull pastures in the summer months, while frogs provide an opportunist crop for rice-harvesters in the wetlands of the Levant.

desserts

flan de naranja

ORANGE CARAMEL CUSTARD

The everyday version of this popular dessert – all Spanish children love it and it's found on every restaurant menu from Bilbao to Cadiz – is usually made with milk and a packet mix. In this sophisticated Valencian version, however, it's made with freshly squeezed orange juice. If you prefer the dairy version, simply replace the orange juice in the recipe with full-cream milk.

Serves 4–6

THE CARAMEL
4 tablespoons caster sugar

THE CUSTARD
500ml freshly squeezed orange juice
3 whole eggs, plus 3 yolks
2 tablespoons sugar

1 Make the caramel in a small pan. Melt the dry sugar, stirring all the time with a wooden spoon, over a steady heat until the sugar caramelizes a rich chestnut brown. This will take only a moment or two.

2 Add 3–4 tablespoons of water off the heat – be careful as it will splutter. Stir over a low flame until you have a thick, dark syrup. Pour this caramel into a soufflé dish or individual moulds, if that's your preference. Tip to coat the base.

3 Heat the oven to 160°C/325°F/Gas 3.Beat together the orange juice, eggs, egg yolks and sugar until well blended. Pour the mixture into the single soufflé dish, or divide it among 4–6 individual moulds.

4 Transfer the mould(s) to a bain-marie (a larger ovenproof dish that will contain water) and pour in enough boiling water to come halfway up the moulds. Transfer to the oven. The large one will need 45–50 minutes, small ones will only need to cook for 25–30 minutes, or until the custard is just set.

5 Allow to cool. Run a knife around the rim and unmould the custards when you are ready to serve. They make their own caramel sauce.

leche frita

CUSTARD FRITTERS

This is Catalonia's sweet version of Andalusia's savoury croqueta: anyone who can make one can confidently tackle the other. Instead of vanilla sugar, you can perfume the custard with scrapings from a short length of vanilla pod or a drop of real vanilla extract. Alternatively, ring the changes with cinnamon, grated orange zest or a splash of your favourite liqueur.

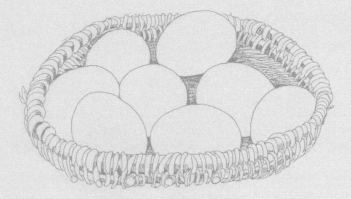

Serves 4–6

6 medium eggs
about 125g plain flour
150ml milk
Zest of ½ lemon
Short cinnamon stick
1 teaspoon orange-flower water or orange juice
125g vanilla sugar

TO COAT
2 eggs
2 tablespoons milk
About 100g finely crushed, toasted breadcrumbs
Oil, for frying

TO FINISH
Ground cinnamon
Sugar

⌒⌒

1 Whisk 2 of the eggs to blend. Mix in as much of the flour as the liquid will accept to make a stiff paste. Whisk another 4 eggs and beat them into the paste, working until smooth.

2 Bring the milk to the boil in a heavy saucepan with the lemon zest and cinnamon stick. Remove from the heat and allow to cool.

3 Whisk in the egg mixture, beating until smooth, and bring gently towards the boil, stirring continuously. Just before it boils, cool it down with the orange-flower water or juice.

4 Stir in the vanilla sugar. Continue to cook gently but without allowing it to boil, until thick enough to set when you drop a blob on a cold saucer.

5 Line a baking tray with clingfilm and pour in a layer of custard as thick as your thumb. Leave to cool, cover with another sheet of clingfilm, and transfer to the fridge to firm for a few hours, or overnight if possible.

6 Cut the custard into bite-sized fingers, squares or triangles for coating. Beat the egg on one plate with their own volume of milk, and spread the breadcrumbs on another plate.

7 Pass the custard shapes first through the egg and milk mixture to coat thoroughly, then press gently into the breadcrumbs, making sure all sides are covered. Check there are no gaps – if so, repair them with a dab of egg and a sprinkle of crumbs.

8 Set them back in the fridge for another hour or so to set the jackets – or freeze until you're ready to cook.

9 Heat a pan of oil for frying. When the oil reaches frying temperature – the surface should be lightly hazed with blue – slip in the custard fritters straight from the fridge, a few at a time so that the oil temperature remains high, and fry, turning them once, until crisp and brown.

10 Remove carefully with a draining spoon and transfer to kitchen paper to drain. Dust with cinnamon and sugar, and serve piping hot, before they lose their crispness.

SERVING SUGGESTION: delicious with a salad of sliced oranges dressed with honey. Or fresh strawberries in season.

coca con almendras y fruta confitada

YEAST CAKE WITH ALMONDS AND CRYSTALLIZED FRUIT

Purists will tell you that the true coca, *as prepared in the Levant and on the Balearic islands, is simply a primitive flat-bread: a flour-and-water dough allowed to ferment in the sun and baked in the embers of a shepherd's camp fire and eaten with oil and salt. Pay no attention; this festive version topped with marzipan and crystallized fruit is much more delicious. You can make it into individual buns if you prefer.*

Serves 6–8

1kg strong bread flour, plus extra for dusting
$\frac{1}{2}$ teaspoon salt
1 tablespoon easy-blend dried yeast
1 teaspoon finely grated lemon zest
4 eggs
100g mild olive oil, plus extra for oiling
250g caster sugar
About 500ml warm milk

THE MARZIPAN
150g ground almonds
150g caster sugar
1 egg yolk

TO FINISH
1 egg, beaten with 1 tablespoon water
2 tablespoons chopped crystallized fruit

1 Sieve the flour with salt into a warm bowl. Mix in the yeast and lemon zest. Make a well in the flour and add the eggs and oil and sugar. Work in enough warm milk to make a soft dough. Knead well until the dough forms a ball which leaves the sides of the bowl clean. Cover with clingfilm – stretch it over the top so that it makes a little warm hothouse with plenty of room for the dough to expand – and leave in a warm place until doubled in size. It will take at least 2 hours: this is a very rich dough that takes longer to rise than a plain dough.

2 Meanwhile, make the marzipan: work the ground almonds and sugar with the egg yolk until you have a soft spreadable paste – you may need a little water.

3 When the dough has doubled in size, knock it back and knead it vigorously to distribute the air bubbles, then form the dough into a ball. Cut the ball into two pieces, knead again and pat or roll out each piece into a long rectangle no thicker than the width of your thumb.

4 Transfer the rectangles to an oiled and flour-dusted baking sheet. Spread each piece with the marzipan, leaving a narrow margin around the edges.

5 To finish, prick the breads in a few places, brush with the egg and water, and sprinkle with the crystallized fruit. Cover with clingfilm and leave to rise again for another 20–30 minutes.

6 Preheat the oven to 180°C/350°F/Gas 4. Bake the breads for 30–40 minutes, until well risen and light. The marzipan will toast and firm – if it looks like burning before the dough has risen, cover with foil. Transfer to a wire rack to cool.

SERVING SUGGESTION: perfect with a chilled glass of *agua de Valencia* – cava on ice with orange juice.

Desserts are only for special occasions. For every day, Spain has such an abundance of fruit all year round that the conclusion of a meal is usually a choice between, say, a slice of melon, a handful of honey-sweet grapes or a juicy orange, a creamy-fleshed custard apple, a ripe fig, yellow-fleshed or rosy-cheeked white peaches, apricots or plums. Summer berries ripen early in the year, making their first appearance in the warm days of spring. Melons are the late summer treat, from the ever-popular honeydew to huge scarlet-fleshed watermelons to the tiny rock melons which can, it seems, suck their sweetness and moisture from a stone. In winter there are quinces, medlars, scarlet-seeded pomegranates, as well as bananas and pineapples from the Canary Islands.

Nevertheless, adults as well as children love sweet things. Oddly for a nation so liberally provided with the real thing, canned fruit in syrup is much appreciated. Children love flan, caramel custard conveniently available in packet form;frozen desserts include an ice cream made with *horchata* (nut milk). A taste for sugary pastries, egg-yolk custards and almond-and-honey sweetmeats can be blamed on the sybaritic Moors: sugar cane was first planted in Andalusia and the Algarve to supply the caliphs' courts with their beloved sherbets and halvas. By the time Granada fell to the Christian kings, the taste was there to stay. After the Reconquest, confections designed to please the ladies of the seraglio became specialities of Christian nuns – prepared to celebrate the feast days of female saints, particularly the Virgin Mary.

pastel de Santiago

ST JAMES'S ALMOND TART

A rich, lemony tart baked to fortify pilgrims on the long walk to Santiago de Compostela, the shrine of St James and one of the three most important places of pilgrimage in the Catholic world, ranking alongside Rome and Jerusalem. The lemon is for the sorrow of Good Friday and the almonds, grown from stock from the Jordan valley, serve as a reminder of the Holy Land. Now you know.

Serves 6–8

THE PASTRY
100g fresh pork lard or unsalted butter
100g caster sugar
1 egg
1 teaspoon ground cinnamon
About 200g plain flour

THE FILLING
8 eggs
500g caster sugar
500g ground almonds
Juice and finely grated zest of 1 lemon
Icing sugar, for dusting

1 Make the pastry first. Beat the lard or butter with the sugar until light and fluffy. Beat in the the egg and cinnamon. Using your hand or the food processor, work in enough flour to make a smooth, softish paste. Work the paste into a ball, cover with clingfilm and leave to firm for 30 minutes. Roll it out very thinly on a floured surface and use to line a tart tin, with a diameter about 22cm. Save any scraps to bake as biscuits – good for dipping into a glass of sweet Malaga wine or a golden *moscatel de Valencia*.

2 Preheat the oven to 200°C/400°F/Gas 6. Now make the filling. Whisk the eggs until light and fluffy, then sprinkle in the sugar spoonful by spoonful, and continue to beat until white and doubled in volume – keep going, even with machinery the process takes longer than you think. Gently fold in the ground almonds, lemon juice and zest. Spoon the mixture into the tart base – it can come right up to the edge because it shrinks as it sets. Don't overfill: if you have any left over, bake it in little madeleine tins or as cupcakes for stray children.

3 Bake for 45–50 minutes, or until the pastry is crisp and the topping firm and beautifully browned.

4 Unmould. When cool, finish with a dusting of icing sugar with, if you have it, a scallop shell printed on the surface (patterns available in Spanish kitchen equipment shops). You can, if you wish, spread a layer of quince paste or damson jam on the tart base before you top it with the almond mixture – if so, give the pastry base 10 minutes in a hot oven first – just long enough to set the surface.

granita de horchata

NUT MILK GRANITA

Horchata, *a legacy of the Moorish presence in Andalusia, is an infusion of crushed nuts and water flavoured with cinnamon and lightly sweetened with sugar. As a thirst-quencher, it's served in a long glass, well iced, and is sold in refreshment bars in southern Spain throughout the summer. When commercially prepared, it's usually made with tiger nuts,* chufas, *although it can as easily be made, as here, with the more delicately flavoured almonds.*

❧

Makes about 1.5 litres

250g blanched almonds
About 2 tablespoons caster sugar (more if you like)
Short cinnamon stick

1 Put the almonds into a liquidizer with a cupful of water (about 300ml) and process to a thick cream. Add enough water to make the volume up to a litre, and leave to infuse overnight.

2 Next day, strain the milky liquid into a saucepan, stir in the sugar and add the cinnamon stick. Bring to the boil and leave to cool. Remove the cinnamon stick.

3 Freeze either in a sorbetiere or in a freezerproof container in the ice-making compartment of the fridge. When almost frozen, liquidize or crush in a food processor to break up the ice crystals. Freeze again until firm.

4 Remove the container from the freezer 10 minutes before you need it, and crush the mixture again before you serve it.

melocotones en vino con canela

PEACHES IN RED WINE WITH CINNAMON

Visually as well as gastronomically dramatic, the peaches acquire a rich burgundy velvet jacket which, when cut open, reveals the golden flesh.

Serves 4

4 large firm yellow-fleshed peaches
1 bottle strong Spanish red wine
5cm cinnamon stick
2 cloves
8 peppercorns
1 bay leaf
About 4 heaped tablespoons caster sugar
Juice of 1 lemon

1 Scald the peaches and remove their skins. Set them in a heavy pan that will just accommodate them.

2 Add the rest of the ingredients: the wine should just about cover the fruit. Bring to the boil, turn down the heat, cover and let the pears poach very gently until tender, about 30–40 minutes.

3 Transfer the fruit to a serving dish. Bring the poaching liquid to the boil and bubble up fiercely until thick, shiny and reduced by half. Strain the syrup over the peaches.

SERVING SUGGESTION: good with *mantecados*, the soft, powdery almond biscuits Spanish children hope to find in their shoes on Twelfth Night, when all good Catholics receive their Christmas presents.

mantecados

SPICED ALMOND SHORTBREADS

These melt-in-the-mouth Christmas cookies – also known as polvorones *(dusty biscuits)* – are a treat for good children when the Three Wise Men come to visit the Christ child on 6 January. The rich powdery shortbread is shortened with lard rather than butter.

Makes about 24

500g pure pork lard
500g caster sugar
4 egg yolks
Juice and finely grated zest of 1 lemon
1kg plain flour
500g ground almonds
1 tablespoon ground cinnamon

1 Beat the lard until it softens, beat in the sugar and whisk until fluffy. Beat in the egg yolks and lemon zest.

2 Sieve in the flour and beat it a little more. Fold in the ground almonds and cinnamon. Add a tablespoonful of lemon juice and work it some more until you have a soft dough.

3 Preheat the oven to 190°C/375°F/Gas 5. Roll out the dough to the thickness of the width of your thumb, and cut out rounds with a small wine glass.

4 Transfer the cookies to a lightly greased baking tray. Bake for 20 minutes, and then reduce the oven down to 180°C/350°F/Gas 4 and bake for another 15–20 minutes, or until the cookies are pale gold.

5 Transfer the cookies carefully to a wire rack to cool – they're very crumbly. Wrap each cookie in a scrap of tissue paper and store in an airtight tin.

helado de chocolate con canela

CHOCOLATE AND CINNAMON ICE CREAM

The ladies of the Spanish court were the first to taste the addictive joys of drinking chocolate, a pleasure unknown in the Old World before Columbus made landfall in the New. The Aztecs considered it an aphrodisiac – with good reason – and in Spain, where it's drunk as a pick-me-up after a night on the tiles, it's usually spiced with cinnamon.

Serves 4

50g best-quality dark chocolate (at least 70% cocoa solids)
1 teaspoon ground cinnamon
2 egg yolks
4 tablespoons condensed milk (or double cream plus
4 tablespoons caster sugar)

1 Break the chocolate into small pieces and soften it very gently over a low heat in a small pan with 150ml hot, not boiling water. As soon as it liquifies, whisk in 450ml hot water. Add the ground cinnamon and whisk until perfectly smooth. Remove from the heat.

2 Beat the egg yolk with the condensed milk (or the cream and sugar), and whisk the mixture into the hot liquid. Stir it over a gentle heat until the mixture thickens enough to coat the back of a wooden spoon.

3 Freeze in an ice cream maker or in the freezer compartment of the fridge until nearly solid. Tip it into a liquidizer and process briefly to break up the ice crystals, and then freeze again.

4 Take the ice cream out 20 minutes or so before you're ready to serve to allow it to soften.

SERVING SUGGESTION: finish each portion, if you like, with a trickle of Pedro Ximenes, the thick, black maple-syrupy sherry made from the grapes of the same name, and a sprinkle of toasted almonds.

biscocho de aceite

MADEIRA CAKE WITH OLIVE OIL

This is a basic four-quarter cake mix – a Madeira cake for which the weight of the eggs dictates the weight of the rest of the other three main ingredients (a medium-sized egg weighs 50g), for which the butter is replaced by the olive oil. Pick a mild rectified oil rather than an extra virgin; if virgin is all that's in your cupboard, heat it to boiling point and allow it to cool again before you use it in the recipe.

Serves 6–8

150g plain flour
2 teaspoons baking powder
½ teaspoon salt
150g light olive oil (not extra virgin), plus extra for oiling
3 eggs, lightly whisked
150g caster sugar
Juice and finely grated zest of 1 small, bitter orange or 1 lemon

1 Preheat the oven to 180°C/350°F/Gas 4. Sieve the flour, baking powder and salt into a large bowl. With a wooden spoon, beat in all the other ingredients until the mixture is smooth and free of lumps. Easy, isn't it?

2 Oil a 1kg loaf tin and line it with greaseproof paper. Tip in the cake mixture and smooth it into the corners.

3 Bake for 50–60 minutes, until the cake is well risen, firm to the finger and has shrunk from the sides. Wait until it cools a little before you tip it out and transfer it to a wire rack to cool. Store in an airtight tin. It's a brilliant keeper as a cut-and-come-again cake.

dulce de membrillo

QUINCE PASTE

*Q*uinces ripen and soften in store, and are ready when you can smell their perfume. This fine preserve is a traditional Christmas treat, usually eaten with a slice of mature Manchego cheese.

∽

Makes about 1kg

2kg ripe quinces
About 1kg preserving sugar
Oil, for oiling

1 Wipe and roughly chop the quinces – don't core or peel them – and put in them in a preserving pan with 1.5 litres water.

2 Bring to the boil, turn down to a steady simmer and cook until the quince flesh is soft – don't boil them too long or they will turn red and the colour of the paste will be too dark.

3 Push the flesh, juice and all, through a sieve. Weigh the pulp and stir in 500g sugar for each 500g of fruit.

4 Put into a pan and bring very gently back to the boil, stirring until all the sugar has completely dissolved. Spread the paste in a very lightly oiled baking tray and leave in a very low oven (110°C/225°F/Gas ¼) to dry out overnight. Alternatively, simmer, stirring throughout, until the pulp pulls away from the sides of the pan, about 30–35 minutes, and then spread it in a baking tray to set.

5 When cool, cut the paste into squares, wrap in greaseproof paper and store in a tin in a dry cupboard. It darkens and firms as it matures.

the
storecupboard

the storecupboard

OLIVE OIL

The defining ingredient of the Spanish kitchen, the rich juice of the olive – an indigenous crop gathered from trees first planted by the colonizing Romans – is used as a finishing ingredient, and an enrichment for the natural juices of a dish, as well as a dressing, and for frying. Spain's oil production is traditionally geared to bulk rather than individual small growers, although this is changing as regional oils with a known and valued provenance have entered the market. Three grades of olive oil are defined: virgin and extra virgin, the uncooked, untreated cold-pressed juice of the fruit; 'refined', which is virgin olive oil which, for some reason, usually too high an acid level, has had to be rectified (treated to make it palatable); and that bearing the simple label 'olive oil', which is a mixture of virgin and refined which may or may not have been extracted as a second pressing with the assistance of a controlled level of heat. There are no rules, but in general the cheaper – refined – oils are best for frying, whereas the virgin oils are good for salads and for stirring into a stew to add richness and flavour. Olive oil enjoys high favour both with gourmets and those concerned with healthy eating, since its polyunsaturated fat is beneficial in reducing cholesterol levels.

SALT

The salt flats of Cadiz and the Balearics have been valued since prehistoric times as a source of sea salt, the main method of conserving fresh meat, fish and dairy products in the days when refrigeration was not an option. Spaniards have a high tolerance of salt, the result, it seems, of the salt-cured olives and pork products which are at heart of the culinary habit; as the diet has improved with prosperity, the consumption of salt-cured hams and sausages, the treats of the Spanish kitchen, have risen. The Spanish housewife likes her salt rough, grainy and unbleached: the crisp crystals give a satisfying crunch to a salad and to the batter for frying as well as a special character to the bread. When preparing traditional dishes that include preserved meats, it's wise to remember not to include extra salt.

SERRANO HAM

Spanish 'mountain ham' is salt cured and wind dried without the application of heat or smoke. Along with olive oil, it is the most valued of flavouring ingredients in Spanish cookery. Its closest equivalent is Italian prosciutto, and its flavour and body are more important than tenderness. The best cuts of ham are sliced off very finely, to be served just as they are. The well-flavoured chewy little bits from near the bone are used to flavour soups, sauces and *croquetas*, or they might be fried with eggs, or go to flavour a tortilla, whereas the bones are sawn up to add richness, along with a piece of the creamy golden fat, to a bean stew.

CHORIZO

A salt-preserved, air-cured sausage flavoured with garlic,
herbs and spices, the most obvious difference between Spanish
chorizo, France's *sausisson sec* and the Italy's salami is the
inclusion of pimentón, Spanish paprika, which adds colour as
well as depth of flavour. Chorizo is also, unlike other similiar
sausages, usually (although not always) lightly smoked. As
with all storecupboard sausages, its origins lie in the need to
preserve those meaty bits of the pig unsuitable for preserving
whole in the form of hams. Chorizos can be eaten fresh and soft
– when they must be cooked – or cured and firm, when the meat
has darkened and the casing has grown a soft white bloom.
When only lightly cured, chorizo is used as a flavouring for
bean stews, or fried and eaten with bread, or cooked with eggs,
scrambled or as a tortilla, in much the same way as eggs and
bacon. The usual flavourings – regional differences are many –
are pimentón, crushed peppercorns, cumin, seed-coriander, red
wine, garlic and oregano.

GARLIC

The unmistakable perfume of this pungent member of the
onion family rises from every Mediterranean cooking pot.
Spanish garlic is mild and sweet, coming to maturity early in
the year, a product of spring rain and early sunshine. When
first harvested, garlic looks like a white onion, a bulb head
whose fleshy layers conceal tiny pearl-like seeds, infant cloves
which swell to maturity by sucking the juice from their casing
until the protective layers are reduced to brittle parchment.
Garlic has a high sugar content, which responds well to gentle
caramelization, although it burns easily. Happily for those who
enjoy its delicate flavour, the garlic press – an instrument which

removes all subtlety from the noble bulb – is not a standard item in the Spanish kitchen. When used as a flavouring for a stew, the cloves are usually included whole, peeled or unpeeled. If the latter, the cooks of Andalusia hold the whole bulb in a naked flame until the papery covering blackens and burns, a process which gently roasts the cloves inside, tinging them with gold. If the garlic is to be eaten raw, the cloves are finely sliced rather than chopped; when used to make a garlic-and-oil sauce, the Catalan *al-i-oli*, they're pounded to mush in a mortar with salt before the oil is incorporated gently, as for a mayonnaise. In Catalonia, *al-i-oli* is eaten as a dip for bread, as a dressing for cooked vegetables, with frittered or grilled fish and with rice dishes that include fish. When blended with pounded nuts and the soaked flesh of dried peppers, the mixture becomes a *salsa romescu* and is eaten in much the same way as a savoury dip for bread; it's indispensable as a sauce for grilled wild garlic and as a dressing for *xato*, a salad of salt fish and bitter leaves. Throughout the region, garlic is used as a cure-all, a panacea for everything from hangovers to the pains of childbirth to the common cold.

Spanish cooks acquired a taste for Moorish spicing in the days when Andalusia was ruled from Baghdad. Although saffron, the sun-dried stamens of *Crocus sativum*, a purple-flowered crocus indigenous to the Mediterranean region, flourished on the central plateau, other spices had to be imported. Supplies of peppercorns, cumin, nutmeg, cloves and cinnamon, imported from the East in the days of the caliphs, vanished from the marketplace when the Muslim empire collapsed and the gates to the East clanged shut. The Christian kings, Ferdinand of Aragón and Isabella of Castile, when faced with a population that had a passion for spices and no way to obtain them, funded a fast-talking foreigner who promised to find a new route. Cristobal Colon (Christopher Columbus) set sail in 1492, the year Granada fell. When the three ships – the *Santa Maria*, the *Pinta* and the *Niña*, none much larger than a modern tugboat – bumped into the New World, although the region failed to yield the familiar aromatics, they found instead chocolate, vanilla and, most important, the chilli pepper. The chilli became a substitute for peppercorns – the most valued flavouring in the medieval spice chest – which delivered the much-desired fieriness and could be grown in the Mediterranean vegetable patch. In Spain, once the fieriness had been bred out to produce mild red peppers, these were left to dry in much the same way as serrano hams, to be torn and added to stews, or, once soaked, the flesh could be scraped from the skin and stirred into a sauce as a substitute for saffron, a labour-intensive (and correspondingly expensive) crop. To this was added the knowledge that dried red peppers, both hot and mild (and which might be lightly smoked) could be milled and stored in powder form as pimentón, and used to colour chorizos and other cured-pork preparations. Among fresh herbs, parsley is the most important, with marjoram, thyme and bay used throughout, both fresh and dried. Mint is partnered with broad beans in the Granada region, tarragon appears in salads in Seville and fresh coriander, appreciated nowhere else in Spain, is used instead of parsley in the hills of Aracena, a result of trade across the border with Portugal, whose sailors picked up the habit while trading with the Orient. Mint and camomile, *manzanilla*, are the most popular of the digestive infusions.

WINE IN COOKING

Although the robust red wines of Valdepeñas and the lighter, more elegant wines of Rioja are used as cooking broths for game and other strong meats, it's the straw-pale, bone-dry white wines of the south – sherry, manzanilla, and the wines of Montilla – which, having a particular affinity with oil and garlic, make a dish distinctively Spanish.

Solera method: White wine, although a perfectly acceptable substitute, doesn't give that peculiarly smoky, oaky, slightly metallic flavour which identifies wines produced by the *solera* method. This method includes a careful blending of wines from one year to the next so that the distinctive flavour is achieved partly by the grapes themselves, partly by the flavour of the oak barrels in which the wine is blended and stored, and partly by the skill of the blender – but the name owes its identity to the method itself.

Sherry: Sherry is always dry in its land of origin, never sweet: sweetness in sherry is only admired when it comes from the Pedro Ximénez grape. Sweet sherries – Bristol Cream and the like – are artificially sweetened to suit the importer's palate. Sherry is used to enliven the cooking broth when poaching white-fleshed fish – hake, bream, monkfish, squid; a splash of sherry in the pan provides the sufficient fragrant steam to open delicate bivalves, which need minimal cooking – clams, mussels, razor shells. In pan-fried dishes such as *pollo al ajillo*, chicken (or rabbit) cooked in olive oil with garlic, sherry is added right at the end to moisten the flesh and soften flavour of garlic. A clear broth such as *sopa de cuarto de hora*, (ham and egg soup), is unthinkable without a dash of sherry, a habit adopted in Britain in the days of Samuel Pepys, a man who liked a glass of sherry in his soup, when the sherry trade was at its most vigorous; consommé with sherry, a combination associated with the days of Empire, remains on the menu in gentlemen's clubs, regimental dinners and wherever Englishmen gather together to celebrate their Englishness.

Dessert wines: Dessert wines such as the sweet golden wines of Valencia, the glossy brown raisin wines of Malaga, the syrupy black Pedro Ximénez sherries of Jerez are traditionally drunk not at the end of the meal but at the beginning, as an aperitif. Whereas the honeyed wines of Valencia are delicious as a moistening liquor for orange-flavoured desserts and the liquorice-scented Ximénez works wonderfully well with chocolate, the wines of Malaga are particularly good in savoury things – adding colour, depth and a touch of caramel sweetness to stews based on the *soffrito*, a gentle softening of onions in lard or olive oil, which gives the slow-cooked stews of Catalonia and the Levant their distinctive character.

OLIVES

To the Spanish way of thinking, olives are inseparable from bread and wine: one without the other two is pointless. Every bar in olive territory, with the possible exception of those in deep tourist country, provides its customers with a little dish of home-pickled olives free of charge. Not least because salt-pickled olives promote thirst while lining the stomach – in theory, keeping the customers sober enough to carry on drinking. Spain's eating olives are gathered while still green and firm (or, if left a little longer, lightly tinged with purple) before they have a chance to ripen to black, the stage at which they're pressed for oil. In Andalusia, the main olive grove region, olives have long been a major export industry: the commercial olive-canners of Seville export pitted and stuffed green olives all over the world. Their canned black olives, however, are the result of deliberate oxidization rather than natural sun-ripening – distinguishing them in texture and flavour from the wrinkled, chewy dry-pickled black olives of Provence or the tree-ripened, brine-pickled black olives of Italy and Greece.

ALMONDS

The Moors planted Spain's almond groves with stock from the Jordan valley – they found the fertile plain of Granada, watered by snow-melt from the Sierra Nevada, ideal for the cultivation of their favourite nut tree. As a result, almonds are used a great deal in the Spanish kitchen, both whole and ground, to thicken sauces and in sweetmeats. Among these, is the Christmas *turron*, a delectable, sandy-textured, almond-and-honey sweetmeat much like the Arab halva, which is made in and around the town of Jijona in Alicante. Other traditional almond sweetmeats include nougats, marzipans and polverones, which are powdery cinnamon-flavoured cookies shortened with lard.

SHERRY VINEGAR

Vinegar is not something any cellarman likes to admit to – particularly those who mature their wines by the open-cask *solera* method – and the vintners of Jerez quietly kept their delicious vinegars for home use, using them to pickle fresh raw anchovies and in *escabeches*, a vinegar-douse which added a little shelf-life to perishable foods – frittered fish, fresh pork – in the days when refrigeration was not an option. It was not until the popularity of Italy's balsamic vinegars – unfermented grape-must which, coincidentally, is also matured by the *solera* method – made specialist vinegar commercially viable. The flavour of sherry vinegar is stronger and more acid than balsamic, with a distinctive spiciness and a rich oaky flavour. Delicious, but best used sparingly; dilute with its own volume of water when using to dress a salad or sharpen a mayonnaise.

CHEESE

Spain has a wide range of cheeses, from the simplest of fresh curds, *queso fresco*, often eaten with honey as a dessert, to sophisticated matured blue-veined cheeses such as Asturia's Cabrales and Idiazabal, a cow's milk cheese made in the Basque Country. Cheese, as the main protein source of the rural poor, is prized in its own right and rarely used in cooking. However, Manchego, the best known of all – a matured hard cheese made from ewe's milk on La Mancha, Spain's high plateau – is sometimes used to flavour croquettes and as a topping for a gratin, although this can be attributed to the French influence rather than anything traditional.

BREAD

Spanish bread has provided the country people with their staple diet since the earliest times. Traditionally it is baked in dry heat in the old bread ovens, and is made with stone ground unbleached flour, sea salt from the salt flats of Cadiz or Mallorca, and pure spring water from the head waters of the broad rivers that water the grain fields. In the rural areas, many *pueblos* still support a village baker who bakes country loaves, rounded in shape for portability, raised with leaven from the day before.

Pan candeal: Rough-textured, chewy and robust, with an elastic, creamy-white crumb and a thick golden brown crust, *pan candeal* (wood-fire bread), is sold by weight rather than volume.

> *Almost everyone agrees about the excellence of Spanish bread. The loaf is very close textured, but it has a taste and sweetness like no other bread in the world. This, I imagine, is because the grain is entirely ripe before being harvested.*

Gerald Brenan, *South from Granada*

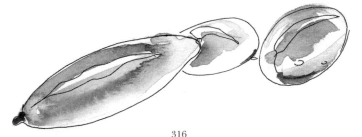

It doesn't grow mouldy but dries to palatable crusts which form the basis of bread puddings and soups such as the rural gazpacho, a bread porridge eaten hot in the winter and cold in the summer.

Migas: Other dry-bread preparations include *migas*, soaked breadcrumbs fried in a little olive oil and flavoured with small amounts of vegetables, cured meats or fish in much the same way as the paella.

Bolillo: The most popular town bread is the torpedo-shaped *bolillo*, a bread roll with a snowy dense-textured crumb and a thick soft brown crust. Shaped like a miniature country loaf – a fat little bolster with pointed ends – the *bolillo* can be comfortably held in the fist and filled with a slice of serrano ham or Manchego cheese, and is often eaten by office workers as a sandwich break and fieldworkers as a midday break.

Saimaza: Breakfast breads include the Mallorcan *saimaza*, snail-shaped buns enriched with lard and sweetened with dried fruits.

Churros: These are tubular doughnuts made with naturally leavened batter fried to order in street kiosks and eaten with steaming cups of coffee or hot chocolate.

LARD

Manteca, pure pork lard, is used in baking and to enrich stews and sauces instead of butter, which is not a traditional ingredient in Spanish cooking. It comes in three different flavours: plain white for pastry and cookies; red (*colorada*), flavoured with garlic, herbs and paprika, to add sparkle to a bean stew; and a paprika-coloured dripping in which small pieces of meat are preserved, a preparation rather like France's *rillettes*, and delicious on bread.

"The first impression [of a Spanish market]
was an almost bewildering sense of the
opulence of natural forces. Heaped all over
the ground, brimming over the sides of the
low stalls, overflowing from great baskets,
were fish of all kinds...every fish I had ever
seen, as well as many other kinds that were
unknown to me – the sword-fish, devil-fish

and ink-fish, of strange shapes and monstrous size. In the upper-room, there were multitudes of vegetables, some fiery-coloured, which glowed in the sunlight. The air seemed to jangle with harsh sounds, and to quiver with bright colours, as the women moved up and down carrying their great baskets. **"**

Christina Gascoigne Hartley, *Spain Revisited*

conversion charts

Use this basic guide for converting measurements from metric and imperial to cup measures. Volumes are standard. Weight can vary according to the density of the ingredients, so the basic ingredients should be used as a rough guide.

USING CUP AND SPOON MEASURES	
All cup and spoon measures should be level (unless otherwise stated).	
¼ teaspoon	1.25ml
½ teaspoon	2.5ml
1 teaspoon	5ml
1 tablespoon	15ml

LIQUID MEASURES		
Metric	**Imperial**	**Cup**
60ml	2fl oz	¼ cup
250ml	8fl oz	1 cup
300ml	½ pint	1¼ cups
350ml	12fl oz	1½ cups
400ml	14fl oz	1¾ cups
475ml	16fl oz	2 cups
600ml	1 pint	2½ cups
750ml	1¼ pints	3 cups
1 litre	1¾ pints	4 cups

WEIGHTS			
Metric	**Imperial**	**Metric**	**Imperial**
100g	¼lb	500g	1lb 2oz
175g	6oz	575g	1¼lb
225g	½lb	675g	1½lb
350g	12oz	800g	1¾lb
450g	1lb	1kg	2¼lb

OVEN TEMPERATURES		
°C	°F	Gas
110	225	¼
120	250	½
140	275	1
150	300	2
160	325	3
180	350	4
190	375	5
200	400	6
220	425	7
230	450	8
250	475	9

BASIC INGREDIENTS	
Cup and Weight Equivalents	
Breadcrumbs, dry	65g / 2½oz = 1 cup
Breadcrumbs, fresh	50g / 2oz = 1 cup
Butter	225g / 8oz = 1 cup
	100g / 8 tablespoons = 1 stick
Cheese, grated Cheddar	100g / 4oz = 1 cup
Iicing sugar	100g / 4oz = 1 cup
Ccornflour	225g / 8oz = 1 cup
Cream cheese, ricotta	225g / 8oz = 1 cup
Flour	100g / 4oz = 1 cup
Honey	225g / 8oz = 1 cup
Parmesan cheese, grated	75g / 3oz = 1 cup
Peas, frozen	100g / 4oz = 1 cup
Polenta	150g / 5oz = 1 cup
Rice, long grain types	200g / 7oz = 1 cup
Sugar, granulated	225g / 8oz = 1 cup (generous)
or caster	200g / 7oz = 1 cup (scant)

bibliography

Andrews, Colman *Catalan Cooking* (Grub Street, 1997)

Aranda, Antonio Garrido (ed) *Cultura Alimentaria Andalucia-America* (Mexico, 1996)

Aris, Pepita *The Spanishwoman's Kitchen* (Seven Dials, 1999)

Borrow, George *The Bible in Spain* (London, 1843)

Brenan, Gerald, *South From Granada* (Hamish Hamilton, 1957)

Calera, Ana Maria *Cocina Valenciana* (Madrid, 1983)

Casas, Penelope *The Foods and Wines of Spain* (New York, 1982)

David, Elizabeth *Mediterranean Food* (London, 1950)

Davidson, Alan *North Atlantic Seafood* (Macmillan, 1979) and *Mediterranean Seafood* (Penguin, 1981)

Davis, Irving *A Catalan Cookery Book* (Prospect 1999)

Epton, Nina *Grapes and Granite* (Cassell, London, 1956)

Feibleman, Peter *The Cooking of Spain and Portugal* (Time Life, 1970)

Fernandez de Alpeiri, Sofia *Cocina y Gastronomia de Castilla y Leon* (Madrid, 1995)

Ford, Richard, *Gatherings From Spain* (London, 1846)

Fraser, Ronald *The Pueblo* (London, 1973)

Graves, Lucia *A Woman Unknown, Voices from a Spanish Life* (Virago, 1999)

Graves, Tomas *Bread and Oil* (Prospect, 2000)

Gray, Patience *Honey from a Weed* (Prospect, 1986)

Hartley, Christina Gascoigne *Spain Revisited* (London, 1911)

Helou, Anissa *Mediterranean Street Food* (Harper Collins, 2002)

Hemingway, Ernest *The Sun Also Rises* (Macmillan, 1995)

Hensbergen, Gijs van *A Taste of Castile* (London, 1992)

Hinde, Thomas S*pain: a personal anthology* (Newnes, London, 1963)

Howells, W.D *Familiar Spanish Travels* (New York, 1913)

Howson, Gerald *The Flamencos of Cadiz Bay* (Hutchison, 1965)

Jenkins, Nancy Harmon *The Essential Mediterranean* (Harper Collins, 2003)

Lladonos i Giro, Josep *Cocina Catalana* (Barcelona, 1992)

Luard, Elisabeth *The Flavours of Andalucia* (Collins & Brown, 1991), *La Ina Book of Tapas* (London, 1989), *The Food of Spain and Portugal* (Kyle Cathie, 2004)

Luard, Nicholas *Andalucia* (London, 1984)

March, Lourdes *El libro de la paella y los arroces* (Madrid, 1985)

Mendel, Janet *Cooking in Spain* (Malaga, 1992)

Millo Casas, Lorenzo *Discurso sobres los origines de la paella* (Valencia, 1987)

Ortiz, Elisabeth Lambert *The Food of Spain and Portugal* (London, 1989)

Pascual, Carlos *Guia Gastronomica de España* (Madrid 1977)

Pitt-Rivers, Julian *The People of the Sierra* (London, 1954)

Porhen, Donn *The Wines and Folk Food of Spain* (Seville, 1972)

Salazar, Valentin & Aurelio *Setas comestibles del pais vasco* (Vitoria, 1985)

Seccion Femenina de Movimiento (ed) *Cocina Regional Española* (Madrid, 1976)

Semler, George *Barcelona walks* (New York, 1992)

Sevilla, Maria Jose *Life and Food in the Basque Country* (London, 1989)

recipe index

general index

acknowledgements

Thanks are due to all those who have instructed and kept me company over the years I lived and travelled in the glorious land I'm proud to call my adopted home, but most particularly to Betty Molesworth Allen, Vicky and Joaquin Cervera, Juan Carlos Barbadillo, Ana and Maria Lobato Ortega, Cristi Lieb, Venetia Parkes, Lorenzo and Clara Larios, Paz Lerma, George and Veronica Lowe, Milet Delme Radcliffe, Maria Jose Sevilla, Sandi Wadsworth, Mark and Priscilla White. To my husband Nicholas and our children – Caspar, Francesca, Poppy and Honey – who kept me company during our years in Spain and shared, with tolerance and patience, what they learned from their schoolmates and elsewhere. To all those who have allowed me to eat at their table or watch them cook and have taken the trouble to answer the damn fool questions recipe-writers ask of those who know exactly how to do what they have been doing all their lives. To my agent, Abner Stein, with whom I have shared many an excellent lunch and who always gives me good advice – most of which I take. My thanks, too, to Ljiljana Baird, my editor at MQP and the source of brilliant ideas and unfailing enthusiasm, to series editor Abi Waters, copy editor Jan Cutler and proof-reader Kathy Steer, all of whom have been unstintingly generous with their editing skills.

Elisabeth Luard has been awarded a string of prizes for her unique, intelligent and engaging food writing. She has been highlighted by food critics and writers internationally as the new Elizabeth David and is considered a Chef's Chef. Mark Bittman called Elisabeth Luard "the best at describing the cuisine of the necessary" in European peasant life in her book European Peasant Cookery. (NYT, 10/13/99)

She has published more than a dozen cookbooks including *Classic French Cooking* and *Sacred Food*, for which she won a coveted Gourmand World Cook Book Award in 2001. She appears frequently on the BBC and writes for *Waitrose Food Illustrated*.